PRAISE FOR DATA DYNAMITE

❝ Dynamite! As the title promises, this book shows how simple tools are liberating data and revolutionizing business, government and our personal lives."
Charles Hoffman, CPA and "Father of XBRL"

❝ David Stephenson is a pioneer in open government data. He has not only grasped the potential for open and contextualized data to reshape business and society for the good, but he has put considerable advocacy effort into making this transformation happen. I applaud the entry of *Data Dynamite* into the expanding body of resources around open data."
Adriel Hampton, co-founder, Gov 2.0 Radio

DATA DYNAMITE

W. DAVID STEPHENSON
How Liberating Information Will Transform Our World

STEPHENSON STRATEGIES

DATA DYNAMITE

ISBN-13 9780983649007

Cover illustration © Chris Jordan, Courtesy of Koepikin Gallery

Book design by SoroDesign
Typsetting Myriad Pro 9/12 combined with the DIN family.

i

Dedication

to

Vivek Kundra,

Chief Information Officer of the United States,

our conversations led to many

of the ideas in this book

and your work is an inspiration

to all who believe in liberating data

and

my wife,

Dr. Rebecca G. Stephenson, D.P.T.

whose support for this project was unwavering

" Comment is free, but facts are sacred."

C.P. Scott, The Guardian

TABLE of

CONTENTS

ACKNOWLEDGEMENTS

Because the topic of data liberation is inherently collaborative, I owe a profound debt of gratitude to the many people who have provided in-valuable inspiration and support.

Ellen Miller and her past and present staff at the Sunlight Foundation, especially John Wonderlich, Clay Johnson, Greg Ellin, and Gabriella Schneider, have been unfailingly supportive. I'm proud that before he became US CIO, I was able to introduce Vivek Kundra to Sunlight. Independently and collaboratively, they have done so much to advance the cause of governmental transparency and liberating data. Five percent of pretax profits of this book will go to support the work of the Sunlight Foundation and its many offshoots.

XBRL plays a prominent role in *Dynamite Data*, and I learned about it from the best—Neal Hannon, who provided incredible insights as well as support; Eric Cohen, a tireless advocate of XBRL GL; Charlie Hoffman, the "father of XBRL"; Diane Mueller; and Mike Willis.

Those who have not adopted social media, and most importantly from my perspective, Twitter, can't appreciate the many diverse and devoted relationships that benefit users such as myself (because of my work and homeland security I was quick to realize that Twitter, by providing real-time location-based updates on user status, could be critical in disasters).[1] Thus I recently found that I was actually user number 262 on Twitter and since then it has become my favorite means of communication. One of the fascinating things about Twitter is that because of the combination of personal and business musings that users post to it you quickly find like-minded people, giving you a good feeling for their interests and values.

The most important Twitter friend who influenced the book is a woman whom I've never met: Wendy Jameson. Early in the project she provided services as a sounding board, provoking me to think outside the box and goading me when I was getting sidetracked. Wendy, CEO of Colnatec, a startup in the sensor field, provided an absolutely critical insight that shaped the entire book: that what I proposed paralleled what Luther had done with liberating the written word. I can't thank her enough!

Many other Twitterati were both invaluable sources of information and support. This by no-means-exhaustive list includes:

From outside the Washington Beltway (some of them so far outside they're on the other side of the world!): Silona Bonewald, Sarah Bourne, Cherissa Burke, Copeland Cassati, Steven Clift, David Fletcher, Dustin Haisler, Dr. John Halamka, Adriel Hampton, Ari Herzog, Tara Hunt, Barbara Milford, Hal Newman, Rose Marie Pena, Angela Siedell, Kathryn Sharp, Rumi Shiraz, Micah Sifry, Alan Silberberg, Luis Suarez, Claudio Luis Vera, Kris Wehrmeister, and Phil Windley.

The Washington Twitterati were simply invaluable both as news sources and for support when things got tough. Among them are Heather Blanchard, Jerry Britto, Andy Carvin, Shaun Dakin, Noel Dickover, Mark Drapeau, Amanda Eamich, Nahum Gershon, Bob Gourley, Dion Hinchcliffe, Hudson Hollister, Alex Howard, Gwynne Kostin, Steve Lunceford, Ron McCredy, Dennis McDonald, Dan Mintz, Doug Neal, Beth Noveck, Steve Radick, Chris Rasmussen, Steve Ressler, Michael Russell, Amy Senger, Lewis Sheppard, Maxine Teller, Andrew Turner, Lovisa Williams and David Witzel.

Christopher Dorobek provided tremendous assistance through Twitter, as editor of *Federal Computer Week*, and later as an on-air host for Federal News Radio, where he interviewed me on numerous occasions.

My first major writing job on the topic was through a contract with Don Tapscott and Anthony Williams of *Wikinomics* fame, to do a white paper for their subscribers on democratizing data.[2]

David Siegel provided tremendous inspiration, as well as content, through his book *Pull: The Power of the Semantic Web to Transform Your Business*.[3] I can't fathom why it isn't a bestseller. You owe it to yourself, pick up a copy ASAP.

Several non-Twitterati who took a strong interest in this book also deserve special mention. Jerry Mechling of the Kennedy School of Government at Harvard frequently gave me access to critical programs where I was able to meet leaders in the field and test my theories on important audiences. John Kamensky, a senior fellow at the IBM Center for the Business of Government, who had been deputy director in Al Gore's Reinventing Government programs, was unfailingly supportive, always asking me for updates and inviting me to be a featured speaker in an IBM webinar on democratizing data. Often on dark days it was fear of letting John down that kept me writing!

My editor, Thomas Hauck, smoothed a lot of rough edges, while SoroDesign did a masterful job of making the book come alive through beautiful design. I was blown away that Chris Jordan was willing to let one of his dramatic data visualizations be featured on the cover.

My mental coaches, Toni Stone of Wonderworks Studio and Dr. Barry Elkin, kept my brain tuned, while my body coaches, Michelle King and Jean Robison, kept the rest of me pumping.

Several extremely generous individuals made contributions that made the editing and design of this book possible, including Eric Bonabeau, Dr. Barry Elkin, Alexander Falk, Adriel Hampton, Robert Hoffmann, Major Alexander Stephenson, and David Witzel.

Last but not least, this book would not have come to fruition without the support of my family, and especially my wife, Dr. Rebecca G. Stephenson, DPT, who literally and figuratively supported me and our family during the time that it took me to complete this book.

PREFACE

It must have been a cosmic irony that I, of all people, should write this book.

Math-challenged to begin with, I had a teacher for eighth and ninth grade Algebra who managed to permanently jaundice my relationship with numerical data. The only pleasurable activity I ever had involving them was figuring batting averages.

Eventually, however, I found that it was critical that I overcome this prejudice, whether for family budgeting or to contribute to public policy debate. Eventually, through the approaches to data detailed in *Data Dynamite*, I came to find dealing with data—in both its numerical and word forms (while most of the data described in this book is numerical, it also can include words)—enjoyable and sometimes even plain fun!

The bottom line: if I can come to love data, believe me, *anyone* can come to love data!

I owe this book, and my involvement in liberating data, to my friend and one-time collaborator, Eric Bonabeau, CEO and chief scientist at Icosystem, Inc.[4] We were meeting in 2007 about an academic paper we were co-authoring on homeland security, when he spun his computer display around, saying, "Here's something I think you'll be interested in." What he showed me was an eye-popping data visualization done by Many Eyes, an IBM subsidiary headed at the time by Martin Wattenberg, the husband of one of Eric's employees. It was such a compelling way to make the data's significance obvious and comprehensible that I was immediately hooked.

Later, Eric also issued the ultimate challenge to me in writing the book: he challenged me by saying, "What matters is if your book makes possible what was impossible before." I hope that I have met that challenge, Eric (and thanks for the financial support to boot!).

From there I began to explore the movement to democratize data,[5] making corporate and governmental information available, plus tools to interpret and work with it, to not just organizational elites but all who could benefit from them. The generally accepted term for widespread access to valuable real-time data, "democratizing data," was the original working title for this book. However, the more I learned about the transformational potential of access to data, the more I felt that democratizing data simply was too passive a term.

I began to speak instead about liberating data, with the vision of an explosion of change just waiting to start. That was the *Data Dynamite* in my new title, with a subtitle of "How Liberating Information Will Transform Our World." That's because, used creatively, real-time data really can transform our work, our government, and our daily lives, as you will see in the pages to come.

One of the first people I met who was active in the democratizing data field was Dmitry Kaechaev, director of the OCTO Lab, a small group within District of Columbia's Office of the Chief Technology Officer (OCTO), charged with planning strategy. Dmitry in turn introduced me to his boss, Vivek Kundra, who was beginning to attract global attention within the liberating data community because of the bold actions that you'll learn more about in Chapter 4.

In September, 2008, Kundra brought me in as a subcontractor on a project to make the District of Columbia the most transparent governmental body in the world. The project was ended prematurely in November that year just after the election because of across-the-board budget cuts, but not before Kundra and I spent several Saturdays in free-wheeling brainstorming sessions that led to many of the themes in this book. I invited Kundra to be the co-author, but he resigned from the project in February 2009, when President Obama named him as the United States' first chief information officer.

Another chapter in this book's history is worth recounting because it illustrates the interest in the technical and business communities in a book making the argument for unleashing data. I met Tim O'Reilly of O'Reilly Media for a nanosecond in the fall of 2008, just long enough to tell him that I was writing a proposal to his company on democratizing data. I heard latter that he and Google CEO Eric Schmidt, two of candidate Obama's first supporters in the tech field, had spent the day together soon after the 2008 election. Somehow the topic of this book came up and within a week (an astonishingly short time in the publishing industry), I had a contract with O'Reilly.

Eventually O'Reilly and I amicably parted company, since their franchise concentrates on tech how-to books and I was adamant in my belief that the liberating data concept was so radical that an evangelistic book such as this one to explain the concept and (hopefully) build enthusiasm for it was needed first, then a wide range of how-to books on topics such as XBRL GL and building data-centric organizations could follow. However, I remain very grateful to Tim O'Reilly and the entire O'Reilly Media organization, including Mike Hendricksen and my editor Laurel Ruma, for their early support.

One thing that Data Dynamite is noticeably short on is specific details on how to implement a comprehensive transition to a data-centric organization. That is intentional, because it would involve specific technological steps that would not be of interest to the general public, an important part of the audience for this book. Watch for a workbook that I will co-author with a noted expert on many of these technologies, which will provide the specifics on how to proceed.

One more important note about style. It will quickly become apparent that I'm not just writing about the topic of data liberation: I feel passionately about it and made it my life's work. Therefore the book includes a number of personal anecdotes about my own experience with the topic and is written in part in the first person to convey my personal involvement and commitment. I sincerely hope by the time you have finished reading this book you will share that sense of passion for the issue.

INTRODUCTION

It was nearly 100 years after Johannes Gutenberg invented the printing press in the 1540s that Martin Luther translated the Bible into the vernacular German, so it could be understood by the general public without depending on priests as intermediaries. He then chose to print that Bible rather than having it hand copied by scribes.

Making the written word accessible to the common man and then capitalizing on this new communications medium ushered in the era of modernity, and triggered a dramatic transformation of commerce and personal growth.

The message of *Data Dynamite* is that, as amazing as everything that has happened in the past twenty years with the Web has been, it is only now that we are ready to fully capitalize on its power, with a transformation as potentially profound as what Luther set in motion.

We are poised to take the next step from *data management to data liberation*, making information accessible to everyone, not just the modern priesthood of statisticians and analysts.

Data Dynamite will make the case for properly "tagged" data having an existence of its own and in the form it was originally entered, independent of any particular application or device that uses the data. More than anything else, this is critical to liberating data. Data must remain available to all rather than being captured by any one application.

The goal is to make *real-time* data universally accessible to all within the reasonable constraints of national security and personal privacy. It's already happening in isolated cases and the results are spectacular.

Data Dynamite will introduce you to revolutionary examples of the liberating-data transformation. One integrates all data to help a state handle natural disasters or terrorist attacks. Another provides emergency room doctors with critical information in life-or-death situations. A third helps patients deal with chronic illness by sharing data with each other and with medical researchers. There are many more, all feasible and affordable.

All of these examples, and more, will be discussed throughout this book. It is very easy for other companies and agencies to launch their own programs of these sorts because these pioneering examples are made possible by free, international, open-source standards for handling data. Many of those developing the new applications intentionally make the code accessible, inviting others to copy and improve on the solutions.

Most chapters conclude with a case study of a company or other organization for which liberating data was literally a matter of life or death, or which faced some other serious challenge where a creative solution was required, on the theory that those for whom the challenge is most dire are likely to create the most creative solution.

As with the Internet and the space program, this is one issue in which government is farther along than the private sector, so we can all learn from government innovations. One chapter is devoted to the District of Columbia's Office of the Chief Technology Officer (OCTO), the organization that perhaps epitomizes the use of liberated data better than any other in government or business at the time of this book's publication. Under former CTO Kundra, OCTO pioneered numerous innovations, including:

→ Publishing a wide range of real-time data streams to invite public scrutiny and allow mashups.[6]

→ Introducing rigor and accountability to project management by treating each project as a "stock."[7]

→ Treating every worker as a "knowledge worker", and giving them real-time data to do their jobs more effectively.[8]

→ Running the precedent-setting "Apps for Democracy" contest which resulted in an astonishing array of crowd-sourced open source applications— and reaped an estimated 4,000% return on the modest investment.[9]

Now that Kundra is the U.S. government's first CIO, his innovations at OCTO will provide valuable clues to the full range of changes he has already begun spreading throughout the US government, especially the Data.gov website, modeled on the District of Columbia's Citywide Data Warehouse. Launched with forty-seven data streams in May 2009, by July 24th of that year, an astounding 100,000 data sets were available on Data.gov, and as of the time this book was completed, the total had soared to more than 270,000.[10]

Those who begin liberating data now can directly benefit from the case studies detailed in the book. The benefits, should other companies and government agencies move quickly to take the basic steps required, will increase exponentially because of the synergies between initiatives worldwide: the "network effects" phenomenon kicks in.[11] Even better, as we will see, some of the most creative and beneficial initiatives can be launched on a shoestring.

Let's get started!

WE WANT OUR DATA—NOW!

IMAGINE:

You're an entrepreneur, making a fortune in the fast-growing Location-Based Services (LBS) industry, which capitalizes on the U.S. Government's Global Positioning Services system.

You're driving when you hit a pothole. In the past, if you wanted to report it to the DPW, you'd have to call them when you got home, and then give them your best guess as to the size of the hole and its exact location. Today, if you live in Boston, all you have to do is put your smart phone on the seat of your car, and if you hit a pothole, the Speed Bump app will sense it and automatically relay the information to the DPW.[12]

Your business is located in the Netherlands, and that means you're lucky. Instead of having to file individual quarterly and annual reports with a whole range of government agencies, you can just submit a single special data file and the information automatically flows to all of the agencies' reports, saving you about twenty-five percent on your compliance costs.[13]

Your dad forgot his heart medicine until he got the GlowCap for his pill bottle. Wirelessly linked to the Internet, it's programmed to glow to remind him to take the pills, tells the doctor precisely when he does take them, and reports to you if he forgets, so you can make a follow-up call. Dad's getting better, and you've got peace of mind.[14]

You live in the small town of Manor, TX, so you can get an instant update on the cost and completion date of public projects by simply taking a picture of a barcode attached to the project sign. The town's government is instantly transparent and accountable.[15]

What makes these diverse, cutting-edge innovations work? Free, real-time, access to valuable data that automatically flows wherever it's needed.

WE LACK ACCESS TO DATA WE NEED

There's something not quite right about our relationship to data.

On one hand, data pervades our lives.[16] Government agencies and companies collect data around the clock about every aspect of our lives, including our births, deaths, education, jobs (or lack thereof), race and gender, spending and saving, and health. Then they use that data to make decisions affecting our incomes, buying options, and even whether we qualify for special benefits.

Data determines how much governmental aid our communities receive.

Data determines which services and products companies will market to us, and where they'll build stores to deliver them, as well as which stores and products they decide to scuttle because data says there's not enough demand.

Data determines where roads will be built. Then our GPS devices use real-time government satellite data to guide us down those roads and help us find new "location-based" services that entrepreneurs create—you guessed it—using that same data!

Data is the basis of medical and scientific research.

On the other hand, for all of data's influence on our lives, you and I have surprisingly little direct access to it ourselves to use as we might need, either on the job or for our personal needs.

That's particularly true with the most valuable type: real-time data. Because it is made available as it is gathered, this data can be used to automate equipment and services and/or help us make better decisions. In the past, technical and cost factors made collecting this kind of data difficult to collect and analyze, and we came to accept historical data as the only real analytical tool. Historical data does let us analyze the past and does have value. But now the barriers to real-time data have been eliminated, helping us make better decisions right now as well as peer into our future.

Despite those benefits, this data is still more likely to remain buried in aptly named data warehouses and be costly and/or difficult to obtain. When we do get it, it's often in a form that is difficult to use, and has to be manually copied every place it could be used.

As you will see, if we did have access to that data, we could do our work more efficiently and cheaply; engage in more productive political debates; and even contribute directly to new ways to deal with some of our era's most pressing problems, such as global warming or health care cost containment.

Yet there's little sense of public concern, and even less outrage, about our relative lack of unfettered access to critical information. Sara Wood, a leader in the movement to make data both available and understandable to the general public, says:

> ❝ *It may not be obvious to everyone, but there exists an important problem of data apathy. No one cares about data. And by no one, we*

mean in the democratic sense…. Good data should affect policy but politicians don't care because they know their voters don't care. People who vote don't care because data is not engaging, not to mention accessible, usable, and relevant to their lives."[17]

Frank DiGiammarino, former vice-president of strategic initiatives at the National Academy for Public Administration and now the Obama Administration's deputy coordinator for recovery implementation, says this is a major problem in the United States:

❝ *We as a country need to treat data as a national asset and resource. It is a valuable commodity but we don't treat it that way. We don't think in terms of where it is. In current structures, it is stove-piped but needs to be moved fluidly… The default question has to be why can't we share it? Data has to become a core component of how government works and how leaders think of dealing with issues."[18]*

However, few care about this issue. Consider this: as you will see in the next chapter, a simple, universal, and free system of systematizing data, which can save companies tremendous amounts of money and streamline their operations, has been available for a decade. Yet you can count on one hand the number of companies that have capitalized on it.

Data apathy is no longer tolerable. Data is so important to our lives that we must all care about data and demand access to it.

MARTIN LUTHER'S INFORMATION REVOLUTION

This is not the first time that humanity has faced information challenges. In the sixteenth century, the written word was inaccessible to all but a few. How that situation changed dramatically and in less than a decade may provide us some valuable insights into how we can speed direct access to data and ways to use it, and the revolutionary change it would bring.

In 1514-5, Martin Luther began to lecture on the Psalms. He had books of devotional readings printed for his students, with wide margins so they could write their own notes. He removed medieval priests' commentaries, forcing the students to interpret the Bible themselves.[19]

In 1517, his 95 Theses attacking the practice of selling indulgences and other forms of corruption in the Roman Catholic Church created controversy and is credited with beginning the Reformation. But equally importantly, six months earlier he had published his first pamphlet,[20] and in hindsight, the means Luther used to spread his Reformation message, the printed word rather than the illuminated manuscript that still dominated theological debate at the time, had as much lasting global impact as the message itself.[21]

That began Luther's efforts to make the Bible directly accessible to the lay public, through printed copies they could own and interpret themselves, instead of having to rely on the priesthood as intermediaries.

Printing and distribution of his revolutionary message was immediately effective, at least as measured by the amount of printed matter. In Germany alone, 390 editions of Luther's works were published just in 1523. By 1525, about three million copies of pamphlets relating to Luther were printed: an astounding number considering the era and the limited number of literate people.[22]

Gutenberg invented the printing press. Luther harnessed its power.

Printing the Bible even changed the very nature of scholarship. As Diarmaid MacCulloch observed in *The Reformation: A History*, there was no longer a need for monks to copy old manuscripts, so they could instead focus on original thinking.[23]

Wendy Jameson, CEO of technology startup ColnaTec, pointed out to me the parallel between Luther's impact and what might happen if we liberate data:

Luther was effective because he both translated the Bible into language that the general public could understand and made it widely available through printed versions. The confluence of transla-

tion and availability enabled the transformation. A literate person in a home or community could now read it to the other community members, the genesis of the empowered layperson.

❝ *The Internet today serves as the analogous means for widespread distribution of data, combined with new tools that make data understandable to everyone. For the first time, data will become a valuable tool for many to whom it was an impenetrable mystery in the past."*[24]

LIBERATING DATA TRIGGERS TRANSFORMATION

The time has come to emulate Luther's example and make data as freely available via the Web as he did with the printed word. Let us call this transformation*liberating data.*

Liberating data makes it automatically available to those who need it, when and where they need it, in forms they can use, and with freedom to use as they choose, while simultaneously protecting security and privacy.

The tools to make it a reality are simple, proven, and, even better, no- or low-cost. All that is missing is the will to change and a grasp of how a relatively simple but admittedly radical shift from current practices and paradigms, away from tight control of information to making it available when and where it is needed (with appropriate security and privacy controls) could make this transformation within a relatively short time.

Since it was never possible before to make data available in this way, the potential for change in every aspect of how we work and live once it is available is profound and pervasive.

THE EIGHT PRINCIPLES OF LIBERATING DATA

Eight principles should guide the process of liberating data:

[1] DATA SHOULD BE FREE

In the past, there were serious problems that made it difficult to gather, process, and disseminate data. As a result, governments and businesses were justified in charging to offset the costs incurred. Today, however, the processes are usually automated, removing that justification.

That data should be free is meant in both an economic and figurative sense. Our tax dollars paid to collect and process most public data. The costs of commercial goods and services also include the cost of data collection and processing, so we have already paid for the data. We shouldn't have to pay again to obtain it.

In a figurative sense, unless there is a valid security or privacy reason, it should also be freely distributed.

[2] DATA SHOULD BE DISTRIBUTED IN REAL TIME

In the past there were legitimate barriers to collecting, processing and disseminating data in real time, so *ex post facto* distribution of the data became the accepted norm. Those barriers have been either removed or will be in the near future, removing the justification for delayed release of the data (assuring data quality was also an issue in the past that can be largely eliminated by steps outlined in *Data Dynamite*).

Data is more usable and valuable when it is available on a data-in-data-out, real-time basis. It can provide "situational awareness" and up-to-the-moment information on fast-changing factors such as traffic, health conditions, or weather, which we need to consider in decision-making. It can also allow automation of many processes that can be triggered and governed by real-time information.

Historical data can be valuable too, and we need access to it as well, but real-time data is at the heart of data liberation.

[3] DATA SHOULD BE AVAILABLE TO ALL WHO NEED IT

Because it was so expensive and time-consuming in the past to collect, process, release, and provide tools to work with, it made sense to only give access to senior management, workers in jobs such as pipeline operation or overseeing assembly lines, or salespeople. Those barriers have now been eliminated or significantly reduced, so relevant data (based on individuals' roles and factors such as their security clearances) should be made available to all who need it in order to help them make better decisions and/or improve their ability to manage and live their own lives. *Every* worker's performance, not just that of certain élites, could be improved if they are treated as "knowledge workers."

[4] DATA SHOULD BE SHARED

When formal or even informal groups of people jointly access and can discuss and analyze data together, the resulting analysis is fundamentally richer and more nuanced than when any individual, no matter how brilliant, works in isolation, because of the diversity of viewpoints and because one person's thoughts sparks a reaction from others. It's time for a little humility on the part of senior executives and others who have traditionally controlled data: when more people are empowered to use it, totally new insights and valuable services emerge. As Professor Nigel Shadbolt, an advisor to the UK's data.gov.uk site said, ".... You don't know if your data set in your department might save someone's day."[25] Equally important, many people and processes can simultaneously act on shared data, rather than having to do it sequentially.

In the past, data created wealth because of its jealously guarded and proprietary nature. In the future, sharing data will create wealth. We must begin to routinely ask, "Where else could this data be used?" This paradigm shift from hoarding to sharing of data will be difficult, but it is inevitable.

[5] WHEN APPROPRIATE, RELEASE REAL-TIME DATA FOR OUTSIDE USE AND SCRUTINY

Government agencies and businesses accumulate vast amounts of data that could be used externally, not only to earn public trust through transparency, but also (especially with real-time and geo-spatial information) to create valuable new services that can complement what the agencies and companies do themselves, or, in its machine-readable form, to drive embedded devices in a wide range of products. That data is also more valuable when it is released in the original, granular form in which it was collected, rather than as interpreted and aggregated by others. Today the default must be to release data. Exceptions to that rule must be justified on substantive grounds.

[6] DATA SHOULD FLOW SEAMLESSLY

Numbers and other data are enriched and become useful information when they are put in context, so the goal should always be to "tag" information the first time it is entered anywhere.

That's a process, explained in more detail in Chapter 2, by which metadata, or information about information, is attached to the data. It's easy to do, by attaching tags to data that give it context and meaning.

A quick overview of tags, how they are created and how they transform data, will be the only technical information you will need to know to understand liberating data and how to make it valuable.

eXtensible Markup Language (XML) and its offshoots, eXtensible Business Reporting Language (XBRL) and Keyhole Markup Language (KML) are three of the important systems of tags that describe the data they bracket and give it meaning, or "structure."[26]

Here is a sample XML file that shows how simply the system works and how easily understood the tags are:

```
<food><name>Belgian Waffles</name><price>5.95</price>
<description>two Belgian Waffles with plenty of maple syrup</
description>
<calories>650</calories></food>
```

....

ILLUSTRATION 1-1: SAMPLE XML FILE
source:

International standards groups agreed upon these tags specifically because they are unambiguous descriptions of various attributes, so they are common sense and immediately understood.

Equally important, tagged data is "machine-readable," which means that computers, control devices and other types of machines can automatically process it without requiring human intervention. Among other benefits, it allows automation of many formerly manual processes, streamlining manufacturing processes, speeding traffic flows, and improving hospital patient care.

When data is tagged, it becomes more valuable because it has context and meaning, rather than being mere numbers or words. It is this form of data transformed and elevated into information by use of tags that will be used throughout this book.

As we will see in the next chapter, if data is tagged immediately the first time it is entered anywhere in the organization, it need never be entered directly again ever (at least hypothetically!). It will automatically and instantly flow wherever the same tags are found, reducing data processing costs and potential error. There will also be a constant stream of data points, rather than few data points that are manually collected and processed, not providing an accurate portrayal of present reality.

[7] MAKE YOUR ORGANIZATION DATA-CENTRIC

In the past, because the tools to distribute and use data were primitive, it was understandable that access to data was primarily second-hand. It was usually warehoused, embedded in proprietary software, and/or interpreted by an élite group of analysts and executives. The data was peripheral to daily operations and often even to long-term projections.

Today, open source software, metadata and other tools allow data to remain independent, accessible to all people and all processes. To fully capitalize on this transition, we must begin to think of organizations revolving around a central core of real-time data.

[8] DON'T VIOLATE PERSONAL PRIVACY AND/OR SECURITY STANDARDS

Establishing the right access standards can mean people ranging from those with no security clearance at all (especially in a disaster situation) to top-secret clearance may all access portions of the same data set based on the situation and their roles, but with widely differing specific levels of access. As we will see in the case of life-or-death medical records, counterintuitively, a comprehensive liberating data strategy should in fact help simplify security and data protection and avoid security and privacy breaches rather than encourage them.

GPS PREVIEWS LIBERATED DATA'S POTENTIAL FOR TRANSFORMATION

It may be hard to visualize how expanding access to real time data would really bring about dramatic change.

To grasp the potential, consider the Global Positioning Systems (GPS), the most common example today of real-time data not just spawning an entirely new industry, but also fundamentally transforming our lives.

It was only in the year 2000 that the US Government stopped intentionally distorting GPS data for civilian use, thereby making possible businesses and services depending on pinpoint accuracy. Location-based services (LBS), just one component of the range of businesses made possible by GPS, have transformed our lives over the past decade, making it easy to travel, find nearby services, and expanded our social networks. They are expected to grow to $13.4 billion in the US alone in 2014, a compound annual growth rate of 51.3%.[27] Can you imagine the potential economic development and quality-of-life opportunities if all of the non-confidential geospatial data compiled by government agencies worldwide was routinely released on a real-time basis?

LIBERATING DATA IS ESSENTIAL TODAY

In the past, the lack of widespread access to real-time data was regrettable.

Given the unprecedented changes facing government, the global economy, and our individual lives today as a result of the continuing global crisis that began in 2008, it is now intolerable.

We need every potential tool and piece of information at our disposal to deal with these conditions and to improve our lives.

If you're a businessperson, given the massive layoffs over the past few years, it is essential that your remaining workers be as efficient and productive as possible. Liberating data will make it possible for the first time to give your entire workforce the raw, real-time information they need to work more effectively. They will also have new tools to help them better analyze that information, and to collaborate to use that information.

Your company will also be able to significantly reduce its non-labor costs when data is liberated. You will be able to improve business process management (BPM) and supply-chain management because all of those who need to coordinate procedures, procurement, and logistics will be able to communicate more readily.

Increasingly in the future, embedded devices[28] will be activated by real-time data, automating previously manual processes, and sensors and other devices will feed a constant stream of data to improve our real-time understanding of conditions.

Data will give us usable information on everything from traffic to our personal carbon footprints to our health conditions in applications and devices that will allow us to act on that data and improve our lives.

SIMPLER, CHEAPER, BETTER REGULATION

In the United States, the federal regulatory system, in shambles after revelations of lax enforcement in the past decade, was at least in part to blame for the sub-prime mortgage scandal and its cascading effects on the overall economy.

Regulation can be reinvigorated through a shift to "smart" regulation, which substitutes a single data file for countless traditional forms. All of the agencies responsible for reviewing a company's operations will be able to share data simultaneously, allowing coordinated review and enforcement for the first time. This should improve the quality of regulatory review and uncover suspicious activities more readily.

The same single-business reporting approach will allow your company to reduce its regulatory compliance costs, perhaps as much as twenty-five percent.[29] By introducing parallel, integrated regulatory systems world-wide based on innovations pioneered by the Netherlands and Australia, we will be able to facilitate world trade and intergovernmental cooperation while protecting the environment, consumers, and workers.

Equally important, government agencies and corporations alike must rebuild public confidence after widespread revelations of shoddy management, lack of oversight, and imprudent investments that brought the global economy to the brink of disaster in 2008. You will be able to do so by liberating data.

How? Demeaning, meaningless platitudes are no longer enough in the face of consumer and voter outrage. Instead, by releasing large amounts of unedited data directly to stockholders, voters and watchdogs, your company can take a "don't trust us, track us" approach, inviting unfettered scrutiny by watchdogs, the media, and the public. Extreme by past standards, only this kind of radical transparency can reassure a skeptical public.

In the United States, the soaring federal budget and deficit led to a political shake-up, and have united the political spectrum to demand less waste and inefficiency, and to open up the legislative process so that the public can be heard.

Vivek Kundra, the former District of Columbia chief technology officer, whom President Obama named the United States' first chief information officer (and who was a co-author of this book when it was originally conceived), calls this approach the "digital public square":

❝ ...*Technological advances now allow people from around the world unfettered access to their government. Through these advances, constituents can hold their government accountable from the privacy of their own homes."*[30]

Making political debate focused more on numbers than emotion might even reduce the amount of *ad hominem* attacks and inflammatory, demeaning rhetoric.

Finally, and perhaps most exciting, liberating data can lead to innovation.

It is now possible, by allowing free access to real-time data streams, to unleash "crowdsourcing" of new services for government and industry alike, better serving diverse groups' needs at low or no cost.[31]

The more organizations embrace this revolution, the more the benefits will multiply. Liberated data inherently fosters linkages and synergies between programs and services that share the same data. Because these programs use global standards, free to everyone, the revolution can and must be global in nature, benefitting nations of all sizes and development status.

STUMBLE SAFELY: THE REVOLUTION IN MICROCOSM

In the pages to follow we will discuss revolutionary examples of the liberating data transformation. One integrates all data to help a state handle natural disasters or terrorist attacks. Another provides emergency room doctors with critical information in life-or-death situations. A third helps patients deal with chronic illness by sharing data with each other and with medical researchers. There are many more, all feasible and affordable.

But to get a basic introduction to liberating data and its power, let's begin with a far more modest example.

To help them and their friends navigate home on foot safely after a convivial evening in bars in the city's Northwest section, a group of young Washington, D.C. application developers developed an app called Stumble Safely. While Stumble Safely wasn't intended to change the world, it actually tells us a lot about liberated data's power to transform every aspect of our lives.

Stumble Safely was an after-hours product of DevelopmentSEED, a leading D.C. web development firm that does ambitious online projects for clients such as the World Bank, the UN Millennium Campaign, and the American Institute of Architects.

It all began in the fall of 2008 when Vivek Kundra announced a first-of-its-kind contest that caught the company's attention.

The D.C. Office of the Chief Technologist's "Apps for Democracy Contest" offered nominal prizes for developers who took one or more of the real-time data feeds that the District of Columbia issues as part of its "Citywide Data Warehouse,"[32] and developed an open-source application that others would be free to use or improve upon and which in some way served the public interest. To encourage creativity, the definition of how the entries served the public interest was intentionally left vague.[33]

Oh, and the teams had only a month to prepare their entries.

The DevelopmentSEED team jokingly called Apps for Democracy "Iron Chef for Developers," referring to the TV show in which chefs are given a limited number of ingredients and length of time to create dishes. Their "ingredients" were the Citywide Data Warehouse data feeds and the time frame the one-month deadline to submit applications.

Given those limits, the team decided to have some fun, and do an entry that they'd like to use themselves.

That's a subtle but critically important part of liberating data. When a wide variety of people not just trained statisticians gain access to important data, they are likely to create applications and other uses based on their personal interests and needs. Compared to when corporate strategists and marketers determine which programs are developed based solely on potential profitability and market share, it inevitably leads to a radical expansion of uses.

According to firm strategist Eric Gundersen, Stumble Safely, which they call a "guide to bars and avoiding crime in NW [Washington]," was an idea that came to the company's staff while working late one night. They thought it would be fun to call attention to some of their favorite bars, while the crime data really might help people avoid being victimized after they left a bar.[34]

As you can see from the screen grab, Stumble Safely is attractive, resembling an aerial view of the neighborhood at night, with large squares that represent popular bars (Stumble Safely is very popular with bartenders because it showcases them and lets users include tips about favorite cocktails!), gray circles that show the location of recent robberies, and red x's that show assaults. Following the map are phone numbers to call a cab (for those who really had too much of a good time!), and the right sidebar lists real-time Twitter Tweets referring to nightlife in the area, reinforcing the message that this isn't just a canned, static map, but a real-time tool.

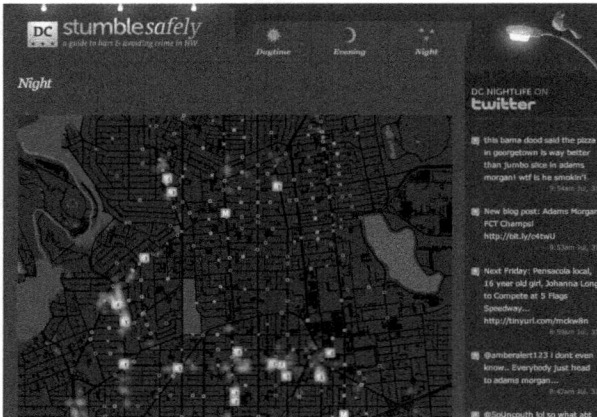

ILLUSTRATION 1-2: STUMBLE SAFELY
Source: DevelopmentSEED

It's cute and fun for pub-crawlers, but a closer analysis of Stumble Safely shows that it combines most of the important elements regarding free access to valuable data that this book will explore, and which underlie much more serious work. They put into practice the principles of data liberation detailed previously.

[1] CREATIVELY USE DATA FORMERLY INACCESSIBLE TO THE PUBLIC

The District of Columbia issues many tagged data feeds from their massive city databases. DevelopmentSEED used six of the feeds, most of which are delivered automatically to the Citywide Data Warehouse as new data is entered, so they are always current.

The names illustrate the wide range of data, especially geo-spatial data, that agencies compile and could be valuable to the public or within agencies as well:

→ D.C. Crime Data

→ D.C. Road Polygons

→ D.C. Liquor Licenses

→ D.C. Water Polygons

→ D.C. Parks

→ D.C. Metro Stations

[2] USE GLOBAL STANDARDS

The D.C. data is valuable because it is identified by a standardized tag system that attaches additional information to the data so it can be recognized and processed by any program or any device that is programmed to draw in that data. As mentioned previously, those tags are based on global standards that are free and accessible to all, which increases their versatility, and makes it easier for others to copy and improve upon pioneering applications.

[3] VISUALIZE DATA & EVALUATE IT COLLABORATIVELY

Most of this data would be incomprehensible to non-statisticians in traditional tabular form. When presented graphically, it instantly becomes understandable to generalists.

Because the DevelopmentSEED staff examined the D.C. data feeds collaboratively, instead of working in isolation, the quality of results improved. When many perspectives examine the same information, the interpretation will be richer and more nuanced than what even the most brilliant individual could accomplish in isolation.

[4] USE OPEN-SOURCE SOFTWARE

Open-source software is usually cheaper than proprietary alternatives, and built on open standards, just as the structured data feeds are. DevelopmentSEED only used open-source applications which in many cases were more powerful than their proprietary equivalents to create Stumble Safely, increasing the ease of other cities adapting the program to local information sources.[35]

[5] CREATE OPEN-SOURCE SOLUTIONS TO ENCOURAGE CONSTANT IMPROVEMENT

One of the contest rules required that the solutions themselves be open source, so that others could copy and/or improve on them. This approach will significantly speed adoption of democratized data solutions worldwide, because other governmental entities that begin to offer the necessary structured data feeds can easily examine and then share or improve on the work of the pioneers.

[6] CREATE MASHUPS

Each data stream by itself would only provide a small part of the information needed to create interesting and informative maps. However, when all six of them were combined, "mashed up",[36] the picture was comprehensive and valuable.

[7] DON'T PREJUDGE WHAT DATA TO NOT RELEASE: SOMEONE MAY FIND IT VALUABLE

You may be tempted to decide that certain data doesn't need to be released because it would be of little interest to others. However, it was combining six of the data feeds that DevelopmentSEED used that made Stumble Safely possible. Some data feeds may be appealing only to a relatively small number of people, but may be invaluable to them[37], so in evaluating a data base for possible release, the default should be to release it unless there are strong privacy or security reasons not to do so.

[8] PARTNER FOR INNOVATION

DevelopmentSEED's Eric Gunderson learned after the Apps for Democracy that Stumble Safely had some unexpected users: the D.C. police. The city administrator told him that the police were using their map to better visualize crime hot spots at different times of day. "This is a great example of a positive externality coming from open data… open data will have many benefits for taxpayers that we can't even imagine now. It is not like the government would have ever paid us to build a drinking site!"[38]

When government agencies or private companies, for that matter, release data, others will use them in creative ways that may create new revenue streams for the company or help a government agency better serve the public interest.

As an added bonus, Gundersen says that the project directly benefited some of their prestigious regular clients:

"The same mapping tools powering the bar site are also being used to help USAID map [food security operations in Africa] and by non-profits like New America to map public health data in the US. In fact it was New America that helped pay for a lot of the mapping work with Drupal that gave us the tools to do this. Everything we do ends up getting reinvested back in. It feels great."[39]

On further examination, Stumble Safely looks like much more than a group of friends' fun little project for themselves and their buddies. It's a harbinger of a new era in which free access to data leads to innovation in every aspect of our lives.

DATA LIBERATION IS CATCHING HOLD

Stumble Safely isn't the only example of liberating data in practice today.

Pioneers in government and industry worldwide are realizing tangible results with innovative data-centric strategies that would have been impossible only a few years ago.

In the Netherlands and Australia, companies now can file a single data file with the government instead of filing the traditional thirty to forty quarterly and annual reports to a wide variety of agencies. The change is possible because all of the agencies have reprogrammed their mandated reports so that they can automatically access relevant data from the unified file. Multiple agencies can examine the company's filing simultaneously, improving the quality of regulatory scrutiny. Participating companies can cut twenty-five percent off of their compliance costs.[40]

Wacoal, the Japanese apparel firm, had thirty-two different legacy IT systems in place, which it had accumulated over a number of years as the company grew through acquisitions. The company went to a new system based on universal access to the same data. As a result, they consolidated their financial reporting, shortened the closing of accounts by two days, and added real-time cash management.[41]

In the District of Columbia, Aki Damme, director of the District of Columbia's IT ServUs team, had to manage a project to buy and install 6,000 computers in city classrooms for a high-visibility new program. The original estimate was that the project would take an entire year to complete. However, an expedited purchasing program plus being able to plan the installations using a Google Maps mashup cut the total length to only seven weeks and saved thousands of dollars in costs.[42]

Agencies responsible for disaster preparedness and response in Alabama can now access "Virtual Alabama," a comprehensive, integrated array of real-time geospatial information, right down to the layout of individual classrooms. It helps them change emergency evacuation routes, know instantly where response vehicles are located, and monitor real-time sensors locating chemical releases and their plumes.[43]

It is very easy for other companies and agencies to launch their own programs of these sorts because these pioneering examples are made possible by free, international, open-source standards for handling data, and many of those developing the new applications intentionally make the code accessible, inviting others to copy and improve on the solutions.

PREVENTING THE 2008 COLLAPSE

You might think you could never have too much beer on hand, just in case the guys drop by to watch the big game in the man cave.

That is, if you haven't played the Beer Game. Created in the 1960s by Jay Forrester, the father of the systems dynamics approach to business, the Beer Game is a simulation that explains how feedback loops, time delays, and information flows affect the way systems function, either positively or negatively.In the Beer Game, *ad hoc* teams assume the roles of key players in the beer sales supply chain: retailers, wholesalers, and bottlers. As they would in real life, each player keeps some inventory on hand to deal with short-term demand fluctuations and/or possible delivery delays. And, as in real life, there's a delay between when more beer is ordered from the next person in the pipeline and when it's received. As the game begins, players start receiving orders from the next player in the loop, but they don't get a full explanation of why they're increasing demand, not unlike what may happen in a business when everyone lacks real-time access to critical data.

Distortions quickly compound. As you probably suspect, as the Beer Game continues, the entire "system," if you can call it that, spirals out of control, huge inventories of stale beer accumulate, and so on.

That's what can happen when we make decisions based on only limited information, and, even worse, when that information isn't delivered on a real-time basis.

Accurate data, delivered exactly when and where you need it, and in forms to facilitate easy use and sharing—is essential to organizations' smooth internal and external operation.

Unfortunately, although the technology now exists to make data available throughout our organizations, only a relatively few organizations have done so. This might have been acceptable in more stable economic times, but the fact that transparent access to real-time data is directly applicable to some of the conditions at the heart of the global economic and political crisis (such as flagging the sub-prime mortgages that were often known only to rogue units in large companies) and to a robust recovery from them makes further delay in making data ubiquitous simply intolerable.

The current reality with many organizations' data is similar to the final scene from *Raiders of the Lost Ark*, when the Ark of the Covenant was boxed up and moved into a government warehouse. There was no dialogue needed in the movie: given how long things can sit in a government warehouse, you knew that was about as safe a location as possible to hide the Ark.

No one was ever going to find it.

Sadly, that out-of-sight-is-out-of-mind mentality can literally be true. In a January, 2009 report, the Army reported that in recent years it had stockpiled an annual average of $3.6 billion worth of excess spare parts in its own warehouses.[45] That's a perfect illustration of the need for free flow of data: if all procurement and materiel specialists had access to real-time data about those parts, they might have been able to put them to work, or at least not buy more. As taxpayers, we all paid and continue to pay a steep price for that type of failure to liberate data.

Too much government and corporate data has been accumulated and stored without actually reaching those who need it and in time to help them do their jobs. Why accumulate all that data if it is not to be put to positive use?

DID PAST OBSTACLES BLIND US TO THE POSSIBILITIES?

In the past, due to serious technical limitations, the problem of lack of free, timely access to data was understandable.

For example, when SEC Chairman Christopher Cox introduced the new regulation requiring publicly-traded companies to begin filing their reports using structured data beginning in 2009, he held up a manually-typed report to the SEC from the 1950s. Cox said that it had been a valuable report in its time, since collecting and reporting data was so hard in that era.[46]

With computerization, new issues such as incompatible databases and applications, and corrupt data were introduced that still restricted access. Even in the rare cases where complete, accurate data is available, users must query the databases in which it resides to retrieve data. More frequently than not, each time the same piece of data is used in a different application, it must be manually re-entered. That slows the process, adds labor costs and increases the risk of errors.

As a staff report of the SEC concluded in early 2009, the current electronic filing system was essentially a document-based one that can be searched but wasn't interactive because the data is trapped in documents, a common complaint about government-mandated reporting formats.[47]

That's a critically important point: in the past, especially when there was no alternative to proprietary software, the data was frequently entered manually into the software and remained there. Today, that is no longer necessary. Data must be available independently of the applications that uses it.

Overall, even though our methods of collecting, storing, and distributing data are more advanced, data still remain inaccessible to most of those who could benefit from it.

As recently as 2005, a highly respected book on data strategy didn't even mention the theoretical possibility of real-time data feeds to every employee as well as to external users. Access to real-time data was still seen as a largely the prerogative of senior management.[48]

Because real-time data feeds were impossible for so long, have we restricted our horizons to the point that, now that real-time access to data is at least potentially available, we can't even appreciate and capitalize on the possibility?

The remainders of this chapter will explore the proven methods that can make real-time data access a reality if we make the strategic decision to do so, and the profound difference that access can make.

ABSENCE OF DATA SHARING A CAUSE OF 2008 COLLAPSE?

We might have been able to condone lack of real-time data access in the past, but became intolerable with the 2008 global economic collapse. Leading accounting experts say lack of easy access to timely data played a major role in causing the problems.

Lane Leskelae, former vice-president of technology programs at The Open Compliance & Ethics Group, blogged at the time:

> 66 *The current economic environment is crying out for sustainable technology standards at the core of information governance. Profound losses in the financial markets were the result of weak governance, failing risk management, and little regard for the consequences.*

> 66 *Many factors contributed to the economic collapse, but the fact that data about the deceptive loan practices wasn't readily available was certainly a major factor, and one that must be eliminated, especially since the tools to do so are readily available.*[49]

Professor Saeed Roohani of Bryant University believes that if a structured-data based reporting system had been in place here in mid-decade,

> 66 *...There would have been little room for mystery about types of portfolios and derived financial instruments that recently failed institutions were holding.... Alarms would have been sounded long before reaching a crisis; the government and stockholders could have taken preventive action."*[50]

As I wrote prior to creation of the Toxic Assets Relief Program (TARP), if all funds received under the program were tagged and automatically disclosed via feeds, then crucial statistics would both flow automatically, and in real time, to federal regulators, as well as to the bank's own staff, helping all of them to do a better job. If the data were scrubbed of any identifiers, because of being tagged it could also automatically flow to public sites, which would allow the public, media and scholars to analyze the data on a real time basis. This transparency would have gone a long way toward building public confidence in the TARP program.[51]

Unfortunately, we have not learned those lessons, so an automatic disclosure requirement was not built into the TARP. The public, media and members of Congress quickly attacked the program because no information was available about how funds were actually spent.[52]

THE KEY: AUTOMATICALLY CONVERT DATA TO INFORMATION

In *Indiana Jones and the Kingdom of the Crystal Skull*, the 2008 sequel to *Raiders of the Lost Ark*, the sanctity of the government warehouse was breached. The Ark of the Covenant, which we thought was lost forever, was found and recovered.

Let's take that as an omen that data too can be retrieved and used!

Today, relatively simple, proven, no- or low-cost tools exist so we can get the data we need, in forms we can work with, and, equally important, on a real-time basis.

TECHNOLOGICAL AND POLITICAL FACTORS DRIVE TRANS-FORMATION

Both technological and political factors make the transition possible and drive it. Three technological components have contributed to the change:

→ The ability to "structure" data to give it context and meaning.

→ The ability to deliver it automatically.

→ Perhaps less obviously, widespread adoption of open-source software.

The following few pages contain the only technical information you will have to master to understand "structured data," the format that is necessary to automatically provide information when and where it is needed. That term refers to data whose meaning is immediately and unambiguously obvious because certain information (referred to as "metadata," or "data about data") is attached to it. Even if you never have to actually perform this operation, it's important that you understand why this works, so please bear with me.

1600: JUST A NUMBER, OR VALUABLE INFORMATION?

What exactly does that number mean? Is it part of the White House's address? Is it the Year San Marino adopted its written constitution? Is it the number of calories in a batch of cookies?

When we see the number 1600 by itself, your guess is as good as mine.

But one simple action takes a number and elevates it into valuable information: "tagging" it. When we read

```
<quantity>1600</quantity>
```

the number's context and meaning is immediately apparent, because of the <quantity> tags bracketing it.

If you've ever clicked "Page Source" on your web browser, you've seen the Hyper-Text Markup Language (HTML) that lets designers "mark up," or format a web page graphically.

Tags that designate how certain content will be presented, such as a pair of tags

```
<h1>News of the Day</h1>
```

designating the size of the headline "News of the Day," may make for pretty displays, but they don't add to your understanding of content.

By contrast, eXtensible Markup Language (XML) and Keyhole Markup Language (KML), for structuring geographic information, are systems of tags that describe the data that they bracket and give it meaning, or "structure."[53]

Compared to cryptic HTML tags such as <h1> and <em>, anyone can understand XML tags such as

```
<name>Belgian Waffles</name>
<price>5.95</price>
<description> two Belgian Waffles with plenty of real maple
syrup</description>
```

Here is a sample XML file using those tags that shows how simply the system works:

```
<menu>
<food>
<name>Belgian Waffles</name>
<price>5.95</price>
<description> two Belgian Waffles with plenty of real maple
syrup</description>
<calories>650</calories>
</food></menu>
```

ILLUSTRATION 2-1: SAMPLE XML FILE
source: http://www.w3schools.com/XML/simple.xml

These tags were agreed upon by international standards groups specifically because they are unambiguous descriptions of various attributes, so they are common-sense and immediately understood.

So how does that apply to you?

If you've ever read a blog, done comparison pricing using a service such as Google Product Search, or used a Google Map, you've benefited from XML and KML's ability to convert data to valuable information. That range of potential applications illustrates an important fact about XML: it's a universal, open standard, available to all,

DATA DYNAMITE: How Liberating Information Will Transform Our World

at no charge, so adopting it is possible for rich and poor, big and little.[54]

I should stress at this point that there is nothing permanently distinctive about XML, KML, or any other specific tagging system. They are likely to be superseded or complemented by other new ones in the future. Instead, it is the concept of the structuring itself that is crucial: using some sort of tool that gives data meaning and context.

Perhaps the most important fact about structured data is that once the tags are attached, they remain attached: the package of metadata and tagged data can flow anywhere and be automatically shared by other applications. That reduces errors, cost and effort, because the data doesn't have to be rekeyed.[55]

As we will discuss later in this chapter, as of June 15, 2011, all publicly-traded companies in the US must now add XBLR (a subset of XML specifically dealing with business terms) tags to their data to meet regulatory requirements of the U.S. Securities and Exchange Commission. For these companies, each additional way they can brainstorm to use the structured data they had to create in other ways (because of structured data's property of automatically flowing wherever the tags are used) amortizes the costs of tagging the data and increases its benefits.

Instead of our old preoccupation with keeping data secret, now the first question we should ask is, "Where else could this data create value?"

DATA THAT'S BEEN TAGGED BECOMES VERY EASY TO SEARCH

Comparison-shopping websites such as Google Product Search work because of tagging. <name> is an XML tag, so if you give the exact name of an appliance you're pricing, your first results will be for that specific one, rather than makes and models that are somewhat alike, because each retailer's listing for the product (if they used XML properly!) would be named and tagged identically.

It can also be used for offline document processing and storage, and, because it is machine-readable, structured data increasingly works with products such as GPS devices, cellphones, and other wireless devices where the real-time data drives valuable content such as traffic information; or it can automate machinery, where the tagged data activates and regulates the equipment.

Because XML is open source, users don't have to deal with expensive proprietary systems that limit the benefits of tagging: the more products or concepts that are tagged, the more valuable each tagged one becomes – it's synergistic. Also, eXtensible means that you can *extend* the system. In the case of specialized needs such as business or health care, international working groups have taken on the task of adding additional tags that meet their specific needs. A group of standardized tags – a schema – are agreed to only after prolonged discussion, review and a formal adoption process. An organization is free to create additional tags for unique internal needs.

I particularly like the way Neal Hannon sums up the transformation possible when data is structured as creation of a data "nugget," because data nuggets become worth their weight in gold to an organization that knows how to exploit their value.

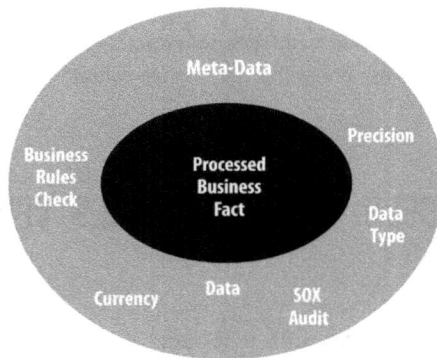

ILLUSTRATION 2-2: THE DATA NUGGET
source: Neal Hannon

"Think of it as a nugget of data coated with extra information that helps explain exactly where it has been and what tests it may have been through," says Neal.

"One could quickly tell if the data complies with various regulatory frameworks, or a manager who's monitoring a procedure for performance could analyze it without having to go back to the original application where it was processed.[56]

XBRL: THE GLOBAL STANDARD FOR BUSINESS TRANS- FORMATION

Of those specialized variations on XML, perhaps the most valuable is XBRL, the eXtensible Business Reporting Language.[57] CPA Charles Hoffman began developing XBRL in 1997. Eventually a worldwide, non-profit consortium of more than 450 major companies, organizations and government agencies refined and standardized it.[58]

Like the other XML schemas, XBRL is an open, license-free standard, usable by all. It automates and speeds processing of business information, very much in line with the data nugget concept. The individual piece of data doesn't have to be manually re-entered each time it is used.

Because it is a standard, XBRL is used worldwide, and can handle data in different languages and accounting standards.

Its usability stems in large part from the fact that typical XBRL tags include the full range of business reporting and accounting terms, such as <NetProfitLoss> <CostofGoodsSold> . In some cases the tags can be added automatically by software, and otherwise adding them is much like doing a typical spreadsheet – with the important difference that the tags are plain English (or other language), not with names such as B4 that you have to remember.[59]

Here is an excerpt from a typical XBRL file. You can quickly see the name of the company, the fact that the currency used for its accounting is the US dollar, and that this particular report deals with the hypothetical company's net costs for furniture and fixtures (<FurnitureAndFixtures>).

```
<xbrl xsi:schemaLocation=" ">
<link:schemaRef xlink:type="simple" xlink:href="HelloWorld.
xsd"/>
<!- Contexts -> + <context id="I-2007"> - <entity>
<identifier scheme="http://www.ExampleCompany.com">Example
Company</identifier> </entity> - <period> <instant>2007-12-31</
instant> </period> </context> <entity> <identifier
scheme="http://www.ExampleCompany.com">Example Company</
identifier> </entity> <!- Units -> -<unit id="U-Monetary">
<measure>iso4217:USD</measure> </unit> <HelloWorld:Furnitu
reAndFixturesNet contextRef="I-2007" unitRef="U-Monetary"
decimals="INF">34457000
</HelloWorld:FurnitureAndFixturesNet>
</xbrl>
```

ILLUSTRATION 2-3 EXCERPT FROM XBRL FILE
source: XBRL Business Information Exchange

More importantly, because it can improve a company's daily operations, not just its reporting, is a second layer of XBRL, XBRL-Global Ledger (XBRL-GL). XBRL itself is primarily for reporting financial results, but GL also covers the data generated in daily operations.

By tagging data with XBRL-GL at the lowest, most granular and operational level (vs. when it might be aggregated with other information) it only needs to be entered once, and then it automatically flows to all other places where those tags may be found, ultimately, to the XBRL reporting functions.

Now that is a data nugget!

In the past, that data would have to be added separately for each operation that used it. Now, with XBRL GL, all of those uses can be closely linked. As XBRL advocates like to say, it provides "a single view of the truth."[60]

RSS SYNDICATION: REAL-TIME DELIVERY MAKES DATA ACTIONABLE

The second critical technical component making liberating data feasible is another XML-based service, automatic distribution of the structured content through RSS (Really Simple Syndication) or Atom feeds.

If we are to realize liberating data's full potential, *automatic* real-time delivery is essential. Any delay in delivery of the data reduces its potential as a tool to assist in real-time decision-making. Similarly, any delay in machine-readable data makes it useless in devices such as GPS: not many of us want to make our driving decisions today based on that traffic jam at eight-thirty yesterday morning!

The most familiar form of data syndication is automated updating of blogs, but the content of automatic feeds can also consist of massive data files. As soon as a value is updated, it is immediately imported into the application, without any further action necessary on the recipient's part.

FROM PROPRIETARY "BATTLESHIP ANALYTICS" TO OPEN-SOURCE

Structuring data and delivering it automatically are the two most important requirements for making liberating data ubiquitous and effortless. Give the data meaning, and get it to users immediately and with no effort on their part!

However, really capitalizing on it requires another, equally pervasive (and highly democratic) evolution: the growing trend away from proprietary software toward open source software, in which source code is made generally available with relaxed or no copyright restrictions.[61]

What is the possible connection between the trend toward open source and liberating data? It's actually critical, because when the data enters proprietary programs, it is processed and coded with proprietary formats, not the standardized, freely available ones such as XML.[62]

To illustrate the problems with what he terms a "Battleship analytics" mentality, Neal Hannon gives an example that anyone who has ever worked with an Excel spreadsheet could appreciate:

> ❝ *The data within applications today is defined by its physical location rather than by its definition or nature. You can see this by looking at the macros in your Excel worksheets, written using cell labels, similar to Battleship, the Milton Bradley game many of us played as kids. For example, "=(C17/C28)" is entered as a current ratio macro. As a result, when additional rows are added to this example worksheet, the relationships of the cells are adjusted and the macro definitions are no longer relevant. Today, analytics are embedded within applications and aren't reusable by other applications or worksheets.*"[63]

That's as contrasted to using structured data, to build the information system around the data, not the application. The structured data can not only be used multiple times but also the user can "… drill down into the data to better understand its origins."[64]

The combination of open source software, with no proprietary restrictions and structured data means that data assumes its rightful role at the center of organizational information management.

I can't emphasize it enough: the concept of data having an existence of its own and in the form it was originally entered, independent of any particular application or device that uses the data, is critical to liberating data. It must remain available to all rather than being captured by any one application.

THE POLICY SHIFT: PUBLIC POLICY DRIVES SHIFT TO-WARD XBRL

The technology innovations that made real-time, structured data feeds possible in turn triggered public policy shifts to capitalize on them.

Once XML and XBRL were available as global, open standards, public policy changes around the world accelerated their adoption, with a particular push from a radical new policy in the Netherlands.

If you ask any business person anywhere in the world what's their biggest gripe dealing with government, beyond taxes the next most frequent answer would probably be regulatory reporting requirements.

Well, anywhere in the world except for the Netherlands and Australia.

That's because in 2007 the Dutch government began offering companies a voluntary alternative to conventional agency-by-agency reports. Instead, it allowed them to file a single XBRL report, under what was called the Dutch Taxonomy Project, a joint venture of the Ministries of Finance and Justice. The goals are both ambitious, and, because they are engineered to capitalize on XBRL's versatility, achievable: to reduce companies' reporting burdens by 25%, or about $515 million yearly.[65]

Like their counterparts worldwide, the average Dutch company must report quarterly and annually to between 30 and 40 government agencies, insurance companies, banks, suppliers and customers. By adopting a standardized XBRL taxonomy (for example, all government agencies now use the same definition of "asset") that can be used to file taxation, financial statements, and economic indicators for all agencies that need it, the project dramatically reduced the number of required data elements that a typical company had to file from 200,000 to 8,000, with no loss of detailed information. While Dutch officials say only about 25% of companies have switched to the new system, it is hard to argue with such a dramatic cost-reporting reduction.[66]

The Australian Federal Treasury is introducing a similar system called Standard Business Reporting (SBR),[67] to unite all state and federal reporting systems. They estimate the initiative will save businesses AU$800 million annually when fully implemented.[68] The more countries follow suit, the more likely a similar system will become a global option: multi-national companies that file XBRL reports for several countries will prefer to do it globally to amortize the time and effort that they've already devoted to tagging the data. Also, the more countries that adopt these systems, the easier it will be for other countries to copy them, because of the ease of adopting open-standard approaches and the reduced learning curve.

THE FDIC'S CENTRAL DATA REPOSITORY PROJECT

By contrast, steps toward implementation of XBRL and a unified reporting system in the US have been more disjointed and limited, reducing the potential benefits to government and business alike. I find this frankly curious, because the results have been so dramatic that they would seem to warrant a more expansive and inclusive approach.

The move toward liberating data in the US began with the Federal Deposit Insurance Corporation (FDIC), which insures deposits in banks and thrift institutions. Of particular importance since the 2008 economic collapse, the FDIC identifies, monitors, and addresses risks to the deposit insurance fund, and attempts to limit the effect on the economy and the financial system when a bank or thrift institution fails. It directly examines and supervises more than 5,000 FDIC-insured banks (more than half of the institutions in the U.S. banking system) and insures deposits in more than 8,700 U.S. banks and thrifts. [69]

XBRL's advantages are demonstrated vividly by the contrast in the quarterly "Call Reports" before and after the FDIC began requiring its use in 2005. The reports cover factors such as a bank's capital reserves and ratios of non-performing loans especially important information to get in a timely fashion given the loss of confidence in the banking system. Banks must submit them 30 to 45 days after the quarter ends.[70]

The data collection and validation process for Call Reports was previously time-consuming and difficult because of issues such as multiple file formats and legacy systems that required manual data entry. Up to thirty percent of reporting institutions submitted inconsistent data, and analysts had to spend up to three weeks manually checking data quality following submission. When there were errors, staffers had to phone, e-mail and fax bankers to ask them to clarify or resubmit data. Combined, these problems resulted in significant delays before the Call Reports could be publicly released, reducing their value.[71]

Typical of XBRL initiatives, the benefits FDIC cites from the new approach include a variety of rather amazing efficiency gains, lower costs, and higher quality data. According to the FDIC,

→ "Ninety-five percent of banks' original filings are "clean," compared to only sixty-six percent under the old system;

→ One hundred percent of data received are meeting mathematical requirements compared to seventy percent under the old system;

→ Data receipt begins less than one day after the calendar quarter-end, compared to weeks of delay under the old system;

→ Publication of the Quarterly Banking Profile, our flagship Call Report summary publication, occurs as much as three weeks earlier than before;

→ Agency analyst productivity has improved ten to thirty-three percent;

→ We gain access to data sooner — improving publishing speed and the ability to analyze data for supervisory purposes; and

→ Regulator and bank use of consistent XBRL taxonomies allows real-time correction capability."[72]

Looking ahead, David Siegel wrote in his book *Pull,* the FDIC might be able to get rid of requiring banks to file the reports if it could be done automatically just as part of doing their daily business![73] Perhaps most important, in light of the Dutch efforts to have all government agencies adopt the common taxonomy, FDIC created a "Community of Practice" for the SEC, IRS and Treasury to share experiences and lessons learned with XBRL. They also held discussions with the U.S. Office of Management and Budget (OMB) to discuss XBRL.[74] Yet, as of 2011, there was still no U.S. unitary reporting option building on the Dutch and Australian models.

THE SEC AND EXTENDING XBRL TO PUBLICLY-TRADED COMPANIES

Following the FDIC's lead, the US Securities and Exchange Commission (SEC) studied XBRL for several years, and began allowing companies to file documents using it on an optional basis beginning in 2005. In December 2008, it adopted a requirement that all documents be filed using XBRL beginning in 2009 for the 500 largest publicly traded companies in the US. Beginning in June 2011, all publicly traded companies must do so.

When the announcement was made, SEC Chairman Cox emphasized that the change wouldn't just affect the SEC's review of corporate performance. Instead, consistent with the wide range of potential uses for XBRL-tagged data, he said it would also help financial analysts and the general public make more informed investment decisions, because they would now be able to make comparisons between companies using the exact same types of data. As he said, "This change will make data universally useful. Instead of buried in ledgers, it will be as free and accessible and findable as any other information on the Internet."[75]

As part of the new regulation, mutual funds must include data tags in filings beginning in 2011, allowing investors to directly compare various companies regarding factors such as objectives and strategies, risks, performance, and costs.

The SEC emphasized transparency and accountability in requiring the change, particularly in light of the mortgage scandal. According to Office of Interactive Disclosure Director David M. Blaszkowsky, "Markets depend on and improve with better information, and even more so in difficult times.[76]

However, Harm Jan Van Burg, who directs the Netherlands' XBRL project, criticizes the US effort because it doesn't require using XBRL for all corporate filings, just for the SEC filings and the FDIC Call Reports. He says the real benefits would have come if the same data file was accepted by the IRS and other agencies, just as all Dutch ones accept it.[77]

CREATING A STRATEGIC DATA POLICY

Once you've mastered data structuring and syndication, you need to create a strategic policy to decide which of your data you will structure and syndicate.

Perhaps the best way to visualize the transformation that can be brought about when data is democratized is to contrast the old linear path, in which data flowed into the data vaults and then only trickled out sporadically and to a relatively small number of users, with an image of a data hub, where the data permanently resides, but is always available to everyone whose role requires access. The access would not be sequentially, or as a gatekeeper filters it, but in the middle of a vast wheel of users who can all share it simultaneously.

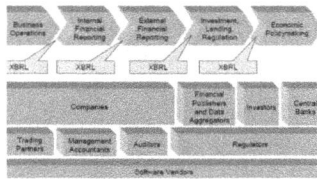

ILLUSTRATION 2-4: (SHOWING XBRL DATA IS CENTRAL TO HITACHI OPERATIONS.)
source: Hitachi Corp.

MOST IMPORTANT, CLEANSE DATA AND ESTABLISH SAFE-GUARDS

Implementing a data-centric process has many facets, but is relatively straightforward and well worth the effort.

It depends, more than anything else, on the data's integrity and on making certain that security and privacy standards are in effect at all times.

One way to improve data integrity and overall operating efficiency is to push for an integrated, all-digital data collection strategy.

When US CIO Vivek Kundra was the District of Columbia's CTO, his agency (OCTO) initiated a comprehensive program to eliminate all use of paper forms and any re-keying of data (as we have seen, structuring data is a vital tool in this regard, since once the data has been tagged, it doesn't need to be re-entered. The data can automatically be entered into any form: the so-called "one version of the truth").

Concerns about data integrity cannot be used as a justification for not launching a liberating data initiative; instead, they are one more reason to make improving data integrity a priority, and, because of the structured data approach, it will actually facilitate data integrity.

CREATE A DATA REVIEW STRATEGY AND CRITERIA

The second step is to perform a methodical review of your data streams. Ideally, that begins with a formal methodology for determining how to evaluate your various potential data streams in terms that make sense for your organization. For example, OCTO plots the potential projects on two axes: those that offer "velocity," i.e., can be implemented rapidly, and, on the other, "complexity," i.e., projects that will take longer to complete but offer compelling value and/or other measure of importance.

Criteria to consider would include data which, if available, would:

➔ Be likely to have the greatest organization-wide value, such as daily gross sales or number of inpatients.

➔ Help deal with chronic problems, such as traffic or supply-chain rationalization.

➔ Be most likely to be "mashed up" into valuable new services by the public, such as location-based information.

David Fletcher, CIO for the State of Utah, suggests that GIS data is an excellent area for government agencies to begin with structuring and releasing feeds, both because they compile so much of it, and because it can lead to so many valuable location-based services (LBS).[78]

DON'T AGGREGATE DATA

An oft-ignored but critical principle is to resist the temptation to aggregate data to help the end user.

Aggregating data makes it less useful. The user is unable to decide for himself or herself what is valuable and what isn't. Any kind of decision to combine the data radically reduces users' ability to create further combinations.

For example, Stumble Safely mashed up six different feeds from the District's City-wide Data Warehouse. If those data streams had arbitrarily been combined before being fed, the value of the information and the opportunities to use it elsewhere would have been dramatically reduced.

Vivek Kundra makes an analogy to the alphabet: "If your basic building block is words, you're limited in how many ways you can combine them. However, if your data feeds are as granular as possible, like the alphabet, then you can combine them in an infinite variety of ways."[79]

DISTRIBUTE IT IN REAL TIME

Generally, anything other than real-time release of data significantly reduces usability. For example, releasing data a year later about a 311 call to replace a malfunctioning traffic light would make of only historical interest. Real-time release allows for creating a map mashup that could actually warn drivers to use caution when approaching the intersection or take a route to avoid it.

There may be valid privacy or security reason for delaying release, but the presumption should be that information is released as soon as it is aggregated, and exemptions must be defended.

THE ULTIMATE TEST: WHEN DATA ACCESS CAN BE LIFE OR DEATH MATTER

When one of my consulting clients faces a new problem, I try to think of another organization that might face the same type of problem but to a far more serious degree. I figure that if an issue is figuratively, or maybe even literally, a matter of life-or-death, then they're more likely to have devoted serious time and money to solving it, compared to another organization for which the problem is merely an irritant.[80]

Applying that logic to data, what organization could have more need for access to accurate, real-time data, while at the same time needing to take extraordinary steps to protect security and privacy, than a hospital?

Boston's Beth Israel Deaconess Hospital (BIDMC)'s Online Medical Record (OMR) is a vivid demonstration of data's power to improve workers' ability to do their jobs and to save lives. Its features illustrate most of the aspects of a liberated-data approach:

➔ Structuring data so it can automatically flow where needed, transformed from mere numbers to "data nuggets.Increasing security by storing data in a unified system, rather than dispersed in variety of places.

➔ Making the organization data-centric, so that all activities revolve around instant access to valuable, actionable information.

➔ Giving varying levels of access to the data depending on an individual's role and data relevant to that role.

Dr. John D. Halamka, M.D., M.S., CIO for CareGroup Health System, the hospital's parent, is in charge of the effort. Halamka, who is also Harvard Medical School's CIO and its dean for technology is a pivotal player in not only nationwide health care information technology but IT in general. Because of his protean energy and vision,[81] he frequently shows up on annual lists of the most important leaders in IT.[82]

Dr. Halamka is also a leading figure in the Obama Administration's efforts (as part of the 2009 economic stimulus program and 2010 health care reform act) to get all medical records online and interchangeable, so what he achieved at Beth Israel Deaconess is likely to serve as a model nationally.

Oh, did I forget to mention he's also an emergency physician at BIDMC, so he knows first-hand how critical data access is to physicians?

Halamka's national clout is also important because, whenever possible, he has tried to pursue integrated data-centric strategies that extend seamlessly from the hospital ER to reimbursement to epidemiology.

In 2007, the Harvard Business School did one of its prestigious case studies, "Information Technology and Clinical Operations at Beth Israel Deaconess Medical Center,"[83] calling it "one of the most sophisticated clinical information systems in the U.S."[84]

Halamka and his 270-person staff emphasize that all of their technology initiatives are designed to support patient care and get the medical staff data when and where they need it in the form they need, rather than to fit IT's preconceptions.[85]

The medical XML data schema that parallels XBRL's use for business is the Continuity of Care Document (CCD).[86] It includes a patient summary with the most important administrative, demographic, and clinical information facts about a patient's healthcare. Information can be forwarded to[87] another practitioner or system to assure continuity of care. It will allow patients themselves to have easy access to records via Microsoft Health Vault or Google Health. As Halamka says, it will make "patient[s] the stewards of their own data."[88]

The Online Medical Record project began in 1996. It became Web-based in 2003, so that the records can be accessed from any computer or handheld with Web access. It includes key records including outpatient notes; medications; lab, radiology, and pathology reports; and hospital discharge summaries, and is used in both inpatient and outpatient settings. Because the data remains in one place and isn't captured or altered by individual applications, it can be accessed simultaneously by multiple users. That, among other things, facilitates collaborative analysis of the patient's condition.

Halamka and his team always focus on the fact that, when it comes to medical data, real-time access to patient data can literally be a matter of life or death. As BIDMC internist Dr. Richard Parker says, "If a patient comes into the ER at 3:00 AM, we'd never know they are allergic to penicillin if that information is buried in a paper chart in the basement."[89]

To put teeth in the Online Medical Record switch, BIDMC required that all its physicians use the system by July 30, 2008.[90]

According to Halamka, the system's benefits include:

➔ Instead of paper charts, stored in an individual provider's files and thus not available for a crisis, the hospital will provide "any time, anywhere availability to all providers."

➔ Secure access.

➔ Helping to improve patient safety through medication reconciliation, communicating test results and immunization records.

Preventive care reminders.

MINIMIZING LIBERATING DATA'S SECURITY AND PRIVACY RISKS

If you are concerned about the security and privacy threats with a liberating data strategy, experts provide reassurance. Dr. Halamka believes that it is easier for the hospital to protect the patient's security and privacy with a centralized OMR than it would be if portions of the record were kept in a variety of databases. When the records are unified, it is possible to design in a number of redundant safeguards, such as requiring that at least two different identifiers are used to make sure the proper record is being used.[91] They also employ other measures to strictly control access to the data, such as determining level of access depending on an individual's role.[92]

Think of the OMR as the acid test of the kind of data nugget discussed earlier in this chapter: the invaluable data remains protected in the patient's Online Medical Record, while those who need it may access the relevant information, including, if need be, many people being able to do so simultaneously. If it works in life-or-death situations such as hospital ERs, what could it do for your organization?

THE DATA REMAINS INACCESSIBLE WITHOUT THE PROPER TOOLS

We have now seen how to create the data streams that can transform companies' and government agencies' internal and external operations, and how to literally and figuratively put that data at the heart of organizations' operations.

In the next chapter we will learn about the tools necessary to capitalize on that data. At that point you will have the basic skill set to liberate data and exploit its full potential. The remainder of *Data Dynamite* will explore how liberated data and those tools will transform government, business and our daily lives.

COLLABORATIVE DATA ANALYSIS

TOOLS TURN DATA INTO INSIGHT AND ACTION

The first time I saw a data visualization, I was hooked.

It was the late 1980s. I had a client who had developed a very primitive (by contemporary standards) software package that took hydrogeologic data on groundwater pollution plumes and portrayed it graphically.

He showed me a stack of data printouts documenting the pollution's location and extent. It was absolutely incomprehensible to me, and I suspect it would have been to most non-hydrogeologists. Then he showed me what happened when the same data was fed into the visualization program: you could see the various geological strata, where the plume originated, where it ended, and how much the size of the plume ebbed and flowed along its course.

It also showed the subterranean plume in relationship to some crude representations of buildings and landmarks on the surface, to put the information in perspective. Yes, you could drill down to examine the relevant data, but the graphics really were worth 1,000 data points: they showed how severe the problem was, where the pollution plume was headed, and where response teams would need to sink shafts to contain and extract the pollutants.

As the client told me, even the hydrogeologists found it was easier to interpret data visually than simply analyzing the reams of data.

Liberating data only gets us halfway toward really creating data-centric organizations. Even if we take measures to structure data and distribute it automatically as detailed in the prior chapter, it is still of little value if we aren't prepared to analyze, discuss, combine, and act on that data.

Data needs to be interpreted and presented. It needs to become *information*.

According to information design consultant Stephen Few,

> ❝ *Numbers are central to our understanding of business performance. They enable us to make informed decisions. The way we measure success in business is almost always based on numbers. We derive great value from the messages that these numbers convey, yet the significance of how we present them is rarely considered.*
>
> ❝ *Contrary to popular wisdom, the data cannot always speak for themselves. Inattention to the design of quantitative communication results in a huge hidden cost to most businesses. Time is wasted struggling to understand the meaning and significance of the numbers – time that could be better spent doing something about them."* [93]

Fortunately, the past decade has witnessed development of an ever-growing range of applications and devices that can help us make sense of data, making it truly valuable. Some of them allow making the data visual, while others allow analyzing them collaboratively. Many of the same factors that influenced the feasibility of data-centric organizations, such as open-source software, Web 2.0, and the systems to structure and distribute data discussed in the past chapter, also led to developing these tools. When combined just as the tools discussed in the last chapter, to structure and automatically distribute data liberates access, these tools liberate its use.

To turn data into information, you no longer need to be an executive with a pricey Business Intelligence (BI) dashboard, or to have a site license for Microsoft Office: you just need web access. But the transformation these tools allow isn't simply one of liberating access to data when it's still fresh and actionable. The change is more fundamental and significant.

The really profound transformation underway due to new data analysis and sharing tools is providing access to data for people to act upon collaboratively, not by just individuals in isolation. For the first time, new technologies allow us to truly collaborate in analyzing, debating, and acting upon data. That collaboration can lead to a degree of wisdom and insight impossible for even the brightest individuals operating in isolation.

DATA VISUALIZATION

That rough visualization of the pollution plume I saw twenty years ago has evolved into a growing array of easy-to-use data visualization tools. As varied as they are, all data visualization tools use graphical means to communicate information clearly and effectively.

Contrast this data on Pennsylvania's share of the 2009 economic stimulus:

	Goal	Program	Dollars
1	CREATE JOBS WITH CLEAN, EFFICIENT, AMERICAN ENERGY	Weatherization Assistance Program	$258,844,698
2	CREATE JOBS WITH CLEAN, EFFICIENT, AMERICAN ENERGY	State Energy Program	$100,783,000
3	CREATE JOBS WITH CLEAN, EFFICIENT, AMERICAN ENERGY	Energy Efficiency and Conservation Block Grants	$114,632,681
4	MODERNIZE ROADS, BRIDGES, TRANSIT AND WATERWAYS	Highway Infrastructure Investment	$1,026,425,012
5	MODERNIZE ROADS, BRIDGES, TRANSIT AND WATERWAYS	Transit Capital	$343,714,184
6	MODERNIZE ROADS, BRIDGES, TRANSIT AND WATERWAYS	Clean Water State Revolving Fund	$155,048,860
7	MODERNIZE ROADS, BRIDGES, TRANSIT AND WATERWAYS	Drinking Water State Revolving Fund	$67,400,000
8	EDUCATION FOR THE 21st CENTURY	Title I Grants	$558,632,364
9	EDUCATION FOR THE 21st CENTURY	IDEA, Part B State Grants	$461,560,769
10	EDUCATION FOR THE 21st CENTURY	Child Care Development Block Grant	$60,146,766
11	EDUCATION FOR THE 21st CENTURY	Head Start	$22,186,572
12	EDUCATION FOR THE 21st CENTURY	Pell Grants	$885,744,567
13	HELP WORKERS HURT BY THE ECONOMY	WIA Training and Employment Services	$92,185,183
14	HELP WORKERS HURT BY THE ECONOMY	UI Benefits Extension	$1,080,572,072

ILLUSTRATION 3-1: PENNSYLVANIA'S SHARE OF 2009 STIMULUS PACKAGE
source: ManyEyes

to this visualization of the same data:

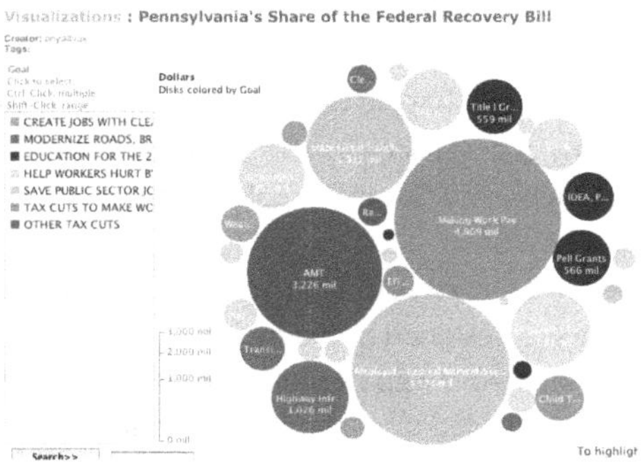

Visualizations : Pennsylvania's Share of the Federal Recovery Bill

....
ILLUSTRATION 3-2: PENNSYLVANIA'S SHARE OF 2009 STIMULUS PACKAGE
source: Many Eyes

Which offers the more understandable, compelling insights into the relative size of the funds the state received for various programs?

Edward Tufte, generally recognized as the person who, through his books and seminars, has driven development of data visualization more than anyone else,[94]echoes what my environmental client said about how even geoscientists are better able to understand reams of pollution data through visual means than data tables:

> ❝ *Modern data graphics can do much more than simply substitute for small statistical tables. At their best, graphics are instruments for reasoning about quantitative information. Often the most effective way to describe, explore and summarize a set of numbers, even a very large set, is to look at pictures of those numbers. Furthermore, of all methods for analyzing and communicating statistical information, well-designed data graphics are usually the simplest and at the same time the most powerful.*❞[95]

DATA ANALYSIS: FROM SOLITARY TO COLLABORATIVE

Charting tools have been built into Microsoft Office and similar proprietary programs for twenty years. However, the past five years has seen a significant evolution in this field, similar to what we have already discussed regarding structuring data, with the advent of open-access web-based programs, including IBM's Many Eyes, Swivel, Yahoo Pipes, and Google Visualization.[96]

They differ in a very important respect from the proprietary programs.[97] Whereas their predecessors were designed primarily for use by individual users, these new visualization programs, being web-based and bundled with Web 2.0 tools such as tags, topic hubs, and threaded discussions, are specifically designed to encourage collaborative analysis.

Researchers call this "social data analysis,"[98] referring to analyzing data in a social, collaborative setting. I prefer to call it "collaborative data analysis," to avoid any misunderstanding that it is about analyzing social data.

FACILITATING AND STIMULATING COLLABORATIVE ANALYSIS

Curiously, humans seem to forget when we come together in an organization or corporation that collaboration should be our default work philosophy: after all, we are organisms and those two terms are both derived from nature. It stands to reason that the same emergent behavior phenomenon that scientists have documented over the past twenty years in other organisms, namely the colony insects such as ants, bees and termites, is probably hard-wired into us through evolution.

Emergent behavior happens when groups come together and can collectively produce results that could not be predicted from the properties and experience of the individual members: i.e., the whole is greater than the sum of its parts. [99]

COLLABORATIVE ANALYSIS TOOLS ENCOURAGE EMER-GENT BEHAVIOR

Tools including Web 2.0 tools such as wikis, tags and topic hubs that encourage collaborative discussion and evaluation of data should increase the chances of this higher level of decision-making taking place, with a resulting improvement in the quality of the decisions.

In a white paper for the CHI 2008 Social Data Analysis Workshop, SAP's Daniella Busse and Richard Hong speculated on how use of these collaborative tools might fundamentally change corporate decision making, away from the current situation in which only specialists analyze and report on data (which, typically, is historical, not real-time), and encourage emergence of the wisdom of crowds. Instead of being the province of élite analysts, the analytics would be embedded in everyone's daily routine activities and would be intuitive, rather than requiring special training. Instead of "sealed-off snapshots," especially of historical data, it would give you real-time insights into current data. Perhaps most important, it would allow the wisdom of crowds to kick in, because of a variety of support tools allowing collaborative analysis and use of the data.[100]

The key will be what Busse & Hong refer to as "embedded analytics," which is consistent with the data-centric approach that frees end users from dependence on specific, costly, proprietary applications, and democratizes decision making by allowing all end users, not just an isolated group of analysts or senior managers, to analyze data and decide how to act on them:

> ❝ *The social interactions are crossing not only multiple communication … but also spaces (conference room, team rooms, discussion forum, focus groups, web-conferencing, wiki). These are becoming perfect media for embedded analytics. The collective thinking, augmented by the new media, is transformed to collective intelligence to guide people to make the right decision."[101]*

Summing it up, it doesn't do any good to liberate data if you don't provide tools so that your entire workforce, not just a few élites, have access to it and can work collaboratively to analyze and act on it.

SWIVEL AND MANY EYES

Two leading web-based visualization sites, Swivel and Many Eyes, illustrate the benefits of combining data visualization and collaborative data analysis.

If you have never used any of these tools, you will quickly find how they tend to draw you in to use of the data and transform your relationship both to it and to other users. In my own case, the first time I used Many Eyes, I was able to scrape the data from a government website, upload it to their data repository, and try a variety of alternative visualization styles, all within an hour, and all without even reading the instruction FAQs! Then I could create a "topic hub" so that all discussions relating to other aspects of this particular issue would be automatically linked and accessible to any user.

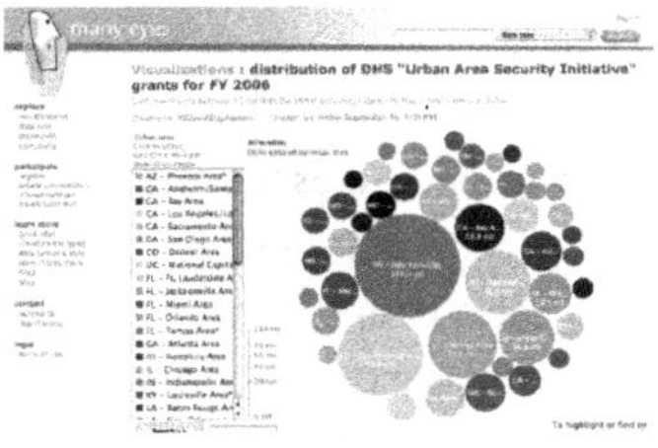

ILLUSTRATION 3-3: MANY EYES VISUALIZATION CREATED BY THE AUTHOR
source: Many Eyes

SWIVEL

Swivel epitomized and facilitated collaborative data analysis. I use the past tense because it went out of business during the summer of 2010. However, I will still discuss it here because Swivel did such pioneering work in the field of collabora-

DATA DYNAMITE: How Liberating Information Will Transform Our World

tive data analysis, even if the management admits they were inept as business people,[102] and in hope that another company will offer its same range of services, especially for organizations behind their firewalls.

The firm described itself not as a data visualization or analysis tool but as "the world's first data sharing tool".[103] Swivel said its mission was to "free data analysis from the silo of desktop software and move it into the realm of the social web".

A white paper by the company's Brent Fitzgerald and Sara Wood describes perfectly, in my opinion, how we need to meld data visualization and social media to transform data analysis and use:

> **"** Swivel operates at the intersection of the emerging world of participatory media and community systems and the traditional fields of business intelligence and data analysis. We aim to foster data availability, accuracy, and understanding of data, which in turn will promote shared insights and new knowledge. … We believe data is most valuable when it's out in the open where everyone can see it, debate it, have fun, and share new insights. Swivel is applying the power of the Web to data so that life gets better. Our approach to this vision is nothing less than reinvention of traditional data infrastructure, visualization, and communication. We aim to free data analysis from the silo of desktop software, and move it into the realm of the social web."10Company officials were adamant that social data analysis is a significant evolution beyond traditional data analysis, and that it was their emphasis on community functions such as sharing opinions, insights and ideas that made the company distinctive.[105]

Swivel featured a variety of proven Web 2.0 tools that encouraged sharing and formation of spontaneous on-line communities and are likely to become commonplace within organizations when data liberation is a reality, including: comments and discussions, ratings, and, perhaps most important, the ability to tag individual data sets and visualizations to make it easier to search and share them. One example is the illustration below, capturing part of a threaded discussion about the significance of voting statistics in Utah:

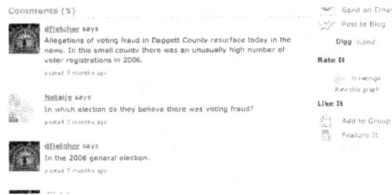

ILLUSTRATION 3-5: SAMPLE SWIVEL DISCUSSION
source: Swivel.com

Swivel also allowed actually annotating an individual data point. The annotation remained attached to the data, and could be turned on or off for all subsequent visualizations or views of that data.

Another reason why I lament Swivel's demise is that it also offered an important service for organizations that understand the benefits of social data analysis and data liberation as part of their data liberation strategy, such as reaching wider audiences and encouraging debate and discussion about data. Instead of waiting for individuals to upload their statistics to Swivel (and perhaps unintentionally or intentionally distort them), organizations could take the initiative by uploading data to Swivel's Official Sources site.[106] A number of US cabinet offices did so (prior to creation of Data.gov, which assumed that responsibility), and, perhaps most noteworthy because of its own mission to encourage debate on economic, environmental and social questions, so did the Paris, France-based Organisation for Economic Co-operation and Development (OECD).

Economists, statisticians, and researchers are OECD's primary users, complemented by students, policy-makers and journalists. In launching projects with Swivel (and Many Eyes), the OECD said that it also wanted to involve "curious citizens, " and that was hard to do with its own sites because they don't allow interactivity. [107]

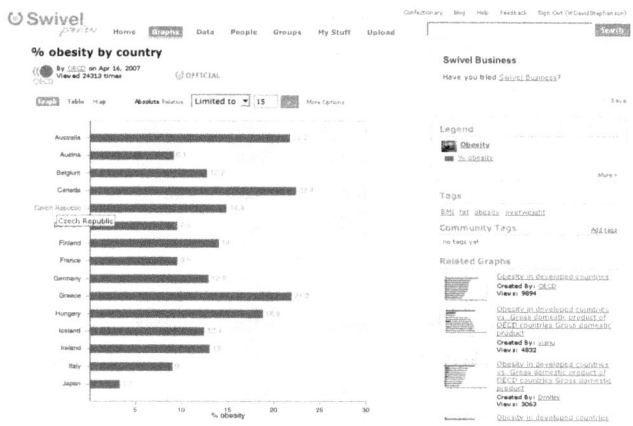

ILLUSTRATION 3-6: SWIVEL OBESITY CHART
source: Swivel.com

MANY EYES

Many Eyes is another data visualization site, with many of the same features as Swivel (in fact, in the collaborative spirit of the field, while competing in some regards, there was frequent theoretical interchange between the two).

As part of IBM, Many Eyes has more resources and its tools tend to be more sophisticated than Swivel's were, but the dedication to the vision of social data analysis is strikingly similar to Swivel's:

> ❝ *Our goal is to 'democratize' visualization and to enable a new social kind of data analysis…All of us…are passionate about the potential of data visualization to spark insight. It is that magical moment we live for: an unwieldy, unyielding data set is transformed into an image on the screen, and suddenly the user can perceive an unexpected pattern. As visualization designers we have witnessed and experienced many of those wondrous sparks. But in recent years, we have become acutely aware that the visualizations and the sparks*

they generate, take on new value in a social setting. Visualization is a
catalyst for discussion and collective insight about data."[108]

Many Eyes co-creator Martin Wattenberg echoes the concerns of Swivel's Sara Wood: "Data is underutilized. We don't know how to deal with it. Visualization is particularly helpful to help lay users understand data."[109]

As you might expect from the director of a site named "Many Eyes," Wattenberg is also a big believer in the importance of sharing the visualizations: "The single most important thing about Many Eyes is that every visualization is linkable. The fact that it can be linked to outside blogs, other visualizations that have the same tags, etc. is really important, because they are shared, which provokes conversation among people about data and their significance."[110]

HANS ROSLING

If popularity is an accurate indicator, the most effective data visualizations are done by the Gapminder foundation in Sweden. The son and daughter-in-law of its director, Hans Rosling, created Trendalyzer, an app that presents data in an animated and interactive way.

Rosling specializes in using these stunning graphics to undermine myths about developing nations ("Show the income distribution of the United States and China over time, and in fifteen to twenty seconds I can make people understand things that textbooks and years of study haven't," he boasts[111]), but he also has a broader mission of using the tool to make data come alive so that people will be more willing to make fact-based decisions.

Rosling describes his mission as a "literacy project," to help non-specialists to be at ease presenting animated data. As he says, "what we're trying to do at the Gapminder foundation, and this is what CEOs want their employees to do, play with data and give it meaning."[112] (Any question about whether Rosling himself has fun with data is answered definitively by his famous TED Talk on global life spans, in which he jumps up to point out key trends, runs back to the mic, and then back to sweep his arm to emphasize another trend[113]!).

ILLUSTRATION 3-7: HANS ROSLING ILLUSTRATES TRENDS IN INFANT MORTALITY
source: Free material from www.gapminder.org

The motion in a Trendalyzer animation is the secret to its success: just putting the time element on the X-axis of a graph doesn't lead to real understanding. When it's represented through motion, you can literally see, for example, that "Bangladesh is reducing its child mortality rate faster than Sweden ever did."[114]

Rosling is beside himself with government agencies that still insist on selling their data:

❝ *Public statistics are owned by taxpayers. These data, which cost about $10 billion in tax money to collect, belong to everyone. And governments are selling them…This hampers entrepreneurs, activists, and politicians from getting access to public statistics. The money is not the only cost; it is cumbersome to pay, it takes time to get the data, and you are not allowed to make the data available to others.*

❝ *Businesses realize that statistics should be free. And there is very strong support from middle-income countries—China, South Africa, Brazil, Mexico. They desperately need statistics because their countries are changing so rapidly and they want to trade. Their entrepreneurs can't afford to pay for data."[115]*

He urged governments everywhere to follow the Obama Administration's stance with the Data.gov site, which not only distributes data free of charge, but is attempting to present it in easily-used formats.

He calls for a three-way division of labor: government organizations who would collect data sets, companies such as Microsoft and Google that come up with new technologies to display the data, and, perhaps most important, "those who 'play' with them and give data meaning. It's like a great concert: you need a Mozart or a Chopin to write wonderful music, then you need the instruments and finally the musicians."[116]

MASHUPS

Data mashups, which combine data from two or more sources into an integrated tool, have familiarized the public with the power of taking various streams of data and combining them to provide value and insight.

The resulting visualization usually goes beyond the original purpose the data was created for: in fact, the new combination might never have occurred to the author of the individual data streams. That's yet another reason for public release of data: when someone with a different skill set and priorities gets access to a data stream, their differing frame of reference and passions will often lead them to see a totally different use for the data than the original author intended.

The most common visual mashups today are built on Google Maps,[117] MapQuest,[118] Microsoft Virtual Earth,[119] or even open source tools such as Mapnik,[120] or OpenStreetView,[121] plus web feeds or, less desirably, data that is "scraped" from the sources when it isn't automatically available in structured form.

An in-depth look at several mashups will illustrate exactly how valuable it can be to combine a wide range of data streams, both real-time and static.

VIRTUAL ALABAMA

One of the most innovative mashups to date resulted from one man's frustration that he couldn't get access in one place to all of the information he needed in an emergency.

Fortunately, that one man was Alabama Governor Robert Riley, and he had the clout to do something about his frustration.

During Hurricane Katrina, Riley was upset: he needed to file a disaster designation application with the federal government, but didn't have access to all the damages assessments he needed to do so. The governor directed the Alabama Department of Homeland Security to pull all of these resources together.

The result was the award-winning Virtual Alabama system.[122]

ILLUSTRATION 3-8-A: DISASTER SCENE SIMULATED ON VIRTUAL ALABAMA
source: Virtual Alabama

It is built on the Google Earth platform, and those associated with the system say Virtual Alabama's most important benefit is that it provides a common operating platform to mash up a growing array of statistical, real-time video, and geospatial information to help officials coordinate response to natural disasters and/or terrorist attacks. [123]

The exact combination of real-time and previously-created data that Virtual Alabama users can bring together depends on the specific challenge at hand, but data elements that can be mashed up range from 3-D models of school buildings (including the floor plans of individual rooms: think how valuable that could be in a situation similar to the VA Tech shootings), gas pipelines, real-time traffic cameras, aerial pollution plumes, locations of fire hydrants, measurements and 3-D models of schools, bridges and other critical structures. In fact, the more that potential users in state government beyond the emergency response community see of the site, the more they suggest adding more data overlays that further increase its utility.

One of the system's first tests came before all components were fully integrated into the system, with the tragic March 2007 tornadoes in Enterprise, Alabama, which killed eight high school students. According to Virtual Alabama Program Manager Chris Johnson, the data for Coffee County (where the strike happened) hadn't even been fully "adjusted" into the system at that point, but the integration of all the elements went flawlessly, significantly improving both emergency response and filing of the federal disaster assistance request.[124]

As often happens with innovative solutions that make data easily available and usable, the benefits haven't stopped with emergency planning and response. Users now include the state's economic development team, environmental enforcement officials, and even law enforcement personnel tracking the locations of registered sex offenders.

NEIGHBORHOOD KNOWLEDGE LOS ANGELES (NKLA)

As important as the transition to collaborative data analysis is in terms of improving data analysis, what's even better is when collaboration can lead to effective joint action.

Neighborhood Knowledge Los Angeles (NKLA) was a collaboration between UCLA and neighborhood activist groups. A pioneer in grassroots use of data, the group began in 2000 to look at how to turn a variety of governmental data sets into action tools.[125]

Their approach was to try to reverse inner-city neighborhood decay through a combination of targeted government programs and private-sector investment.

A key was to objectively identify areas in need of intervention by using an approach created by the Center for Neighborhood Technology as part of its "Neighborhood Early Warning System" (NEWS). The system tracks a variety of indicators of problems that can result in urban decay, including property tax and public utility arrears, housing code violations, utility shutoffs, public abatements, and tax sales. Typically, different city departments collect each of these data. In the past, a given home might have appeared in the data for each indicator without city officials in other departments being aware of the seriousness of the threat.

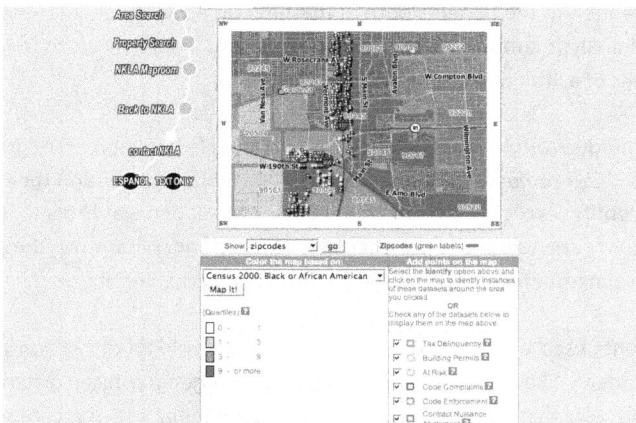

ILLUSTRATION 3-8-B: NEIGHBORHOOD KNOWLEDGE LA "NEWS" MASHUP
source: Neighborhood Knowledge LA

As the above illustration shows, NKLA gave each of the indicators a different color, and mashed the data from all seven factors onto a map. This "20,000-foot view" was chosen specifically to illustrate that while there might be individual signs of decay of one sort or another in some of the outlying blocks (not visible in this remote a view), the most troubled blocks are all very clear and clustered together. If you were to click on one of the colored rectangles for a given block, you could see the underlying data, but in one sense that really isn't needed: simply seeing some blocks that look like patchwork quilts, with all seven factors found repeatedly, is an instant alarm that the various city agencies (plus civic groups such as NKLA) need to launch a coordinated program to leverage all of their resources in combination to save the neighborhood. [126]

Thus, shared access to data may not only lead to better analysis of the data, but also to collaborative action as well.

THE SEARCH FOR OSAMA BIN LADEN

Another UCLA academic mashup project gained global notoriety in 2009, and called attention to the benefits both of mashing up a variety of databases and using social analytic tools to harvest numerous users' insights (not to mention the advantages of a little outside-the-box thinking!).

Using techniques originally developed to chart wildlife habitats and migration patterns, two UCLA professors, Thomas Gillespie and John Agnew, and their students tried to identify places in Pakistan where Osama bin Laden was likely to hide. After all, as one wry analysis of the project observed, "bin Laden has everything in common with a member of a species trying to escape extinction."[127]

The students used a number of theories regarding wildlife dispersion to zero in on bin Laden's likely location. "For example, bio-geographical distance-decay theory suggests that as we look further from some initial site, the composition of an ecosystem will change exponentially. So, the further bin Laden gets from his last known location in Pakistan, the less he'll like the demographics"[128]in fact, he'd probably find himself in the more secular, non-Taliban regions of Pakistan, significantly increasing the chances someone would turn him in for reward money.

Having limited the probable range of areas bin Laden would consider safe, the UCLA research team added in other factors from known facts about bin Laden (I suspect each mashed up another layer of data) to narrow the range of possible hideouts:

→ He'd need to be near reliable electrical supplies (because he's reportedly on dialysis)

→ He'd be uncomfortable on low-ceilinged buildings, since he's 6'4"

→ Having survived several near-misses from Predator drones, he wants to be sheltered from the chance of being identified by satellites, so a tree-lined site is preferable.

Ultimately, they narrowed down the likely hiding places to one of three buildings in Parachinar, in the Kurram tribal region near Afghanistan! After his targeted assassination, we now know that wasn't where bin Laden was hiding, but his compound did meet two of the three criteria.

Given this example, can you imagine the kinds of variations on this project that will become commonplace when mashups become second-nature to us?

ILLUSTRATION 3-9: 3 POSSIBLE HIDING PLACES FOR OSAMA BIN LADEN
source: UCLA

DASHBOARDS

For the last decade or so, business élites such as senior management and sales have been using business intelligence (BI) dashboards. These are applications that give users simultaneous access (including visualizations) to a variety of data streams such as sales, inventory, and operating information. However, the price of these systems, the difficulty of use, and the length of time required to configure and get a BI server running has been an obstacle to full-scale deployment throughout many organizations, so traditional business intelligence dashboards have not encouraged liberating data.

In the past few years, a growing number of cloud-based dashboards have become available, dramatically reducing costs, as well as integrating better into a data-centric strategy (vs. the Battleship analytics model discussed in the previous chapter).

A good example is Tableau, whose clients include the District of Columbia, Google, Apple, Coca Cola, the US Air Force, and Walmart. In an early 2009 podcast, Tableau CEO Christian Chabot contrasted the upstarts' vision, very much consistent with liberating data and empowering the entire workforce, with traditional BI powerhouses such as Cognos, Business Objects, and Hyperion, which he said are "entering their sunset years because of their approach." He said that BI platforms have tended to centralize decision-making, and reports are typically prepared by BI experts, so users don't get to play directly with the data. Since it's the BI analysts who create the reports, there's always a delay in getting reports until the specialists can generate them.[129]

This is exactly the kind of centralized, top-down approach that is rendered obsolete by liberating data and affordable tools to work with it!

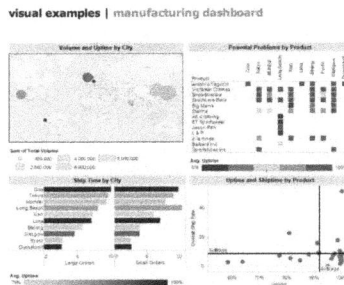

visual examples | manufacturing dashboard

ILLUSTRATION 3-10: TABLEAU BI DASHBOARD FOR CLOTHING MANUFACTURER
source: Tableau Software

By contrast, Tableau's dashboard (and competitors such as Visokio) are easily mastered by end users. Its web-based Tableau Server can be installed in minutes and allows customers to extend dashboard access to their entire workforce. It encourages social data analysis because anyone can participate in online discussions, add tags, notes, ask questions, or offer an opinion.

DATA DYNAMITE: How Liberating Information Will Transform Our World

WHEN ANALYZING DATA IS MATTER OF LIFE AND DEATH: TIES

The previous chapter concluded with the example of how Beth Israel Deaconess Hospital uses its Online Medical Records, because access to real-time data is of life-or-death importance for individual patients in hospitals.

On a larger scale, disaster management is the acid test for collaborative data analysis and decision making, because it typically requires that a wide range of participants simultaneously consider the full range of available data, including:

→ Real-time video

→ Geographic information mashups

→ Threaded discussions

→ Real-time voice

→ Advance planning documents

Just as hospitals must constantly balance the need for security and privacy safeguards with the equally compelling need for access to all available data about the individual patient by approved users such as emergency room physicians, the emergency management system must constantly balance, as CEO Charles Jennings of Swan Island Networks puts it, the paradox of "open yet trusted: information wants to be free, but in a crisis it also helps if it is correct."

After 9/11, Jennings and Swan Island Networks co-founder Pete O'Dell began tackling the open-yet-trusted problem. Long familiar with emergent behavior, they advocated using a swarm intelligence model to build systems that were both dynamic and open, and had stiff information assurance controls.

The result was Swan Island's Trusted Information Exchange Service, or TIES®, a cloud-based application.

As with the Beth Israel Deaconess Medical Center (BIDMC) Online Medical Record system, the key is another form of structured, automatically-delivered data. Another XML schema, the Common Alerting Protocol (CAP), is a data format specifically created to exchange public warnings and emergency information between alerting technologies and emergency managers and responders. Because it is data-centric, rather than dictated by various applications, CAP allows consistent delivery of warning messages over many devices and to many applications.[130]

TIES uses CAP (plus RSS, KML and other standards) to create a kind of super mashup. Because effective emergency management requires fusing every available form of "situational awareness," it can combine information feeds from many sources (both open and private/sensitive) to create a fused, layered situational awareness picture.

As with emergency medicine, historical data by itself is inadequate in a disaster or terrorism situation. TIES collects real-time information to present a minute-by-minute picture of what's happening—globally or locally.

TIES is the ultimate in data-centric convergence. It can integrate a wide range of Web 2.0 and other real-time and static data sources including 911 data, Twitter, confidential internal corporate bulletins, critical infrastructure locations, facility security, global terror alerts and earthquake alerts, and many more, because much of the information is in the form of structured data.

TIES presents this fused information in a series of user-customizable dashboards, each of which consists of many different kinds of widgets. These widgets range from dynamic maps and text alerts to collaboration tools.

ILLUSTRATION 3-11: SAMPLE TIES DASHBOARD
source: Swan Island Networks

TIES's most unique feature is its community of trust authorization architecture, not unlike the wide variety of role-based dashboards that Dr. Halamka offers BIDMC users. TIES's dashboards can be self-created by each user or distributed as read-only "information products" to a community of users or even subcommunities that may have access to certain data not available to the overall community. (For example, one TIES Fortune 500 customer has a general community for all its employees, and a much smaller group sharing sensitive information about employee violence and response).

A NEW KIND OF DECISION-MAKING

Emergency management doesn't allow the luxury of calm, deliberate decision making.

Instead, and similar to emergency medicine, it requires using the information available at the time to make decisions, which may have to be radically altered only minutes later as newer data is received and analyzed.

For example, Major John Bennett of the Tampa Police Department used TIES for Super Bowl XLIII, for which he was incident commander. TIES provided a geospatially-based situational awareness picture integrating real-time 911 alerts, real-time radar weather and traffic reports, and webcams throughout the stadium and region. It mashed up these feeds and displayed them on dashboards accessed with a browser.[131]

Most companies don't face this kind of critical real-time decision-making challenge. However, the structured data tagged with metadata using the Common Alerting Protocol and delivered automatically via RSS, combined with the Web 2.0 communication and analysis tools offered by the TIES dashboard, can make emergency management the laboratory for innovative new approaches to democratized organizational decision-making that companies facing less intensive needs can now consider implementing as the same resources become available to them.

Harkening back to the discussion of collaborative data analysis earlier in this chapter, the result of analyzing data collectively using TIES in a crisis makes the resulting decision-making more collegial.

The likely result will be better decisions because the emergency planners and first responders will have access to actionable information when they really need it, and the interplay of various types of expertise, various perspectives, and various personalities will mean that the decisions will have been more thoroughly discussed and more potential pitfalls uncovered before the decision is reached, rather than after.

As James Surowieki wrote in *The Wisdom of Crowds*,

> **❝** *What is demonstrably true of some of these groups namely, that they are smart and good at problem solving is potentially true of most, if not all of them...If you put together a big enough and diverse enough group of people and ask them to 'make decisions affecting matters of general interest,' that group's decisions will, over time, be 'intellectually [superior] to the isolated individual,' no matter how smart or well-informed he is."* [132]

DYNAMITE COMBINATION: REAL-TIME DATA + GROUP INSIGHTS

The potential of data to dynamite current practices referred to in the title depends on both the availability of the real-time data and the collaborative tools to analyze and act on it.

Combined, they mean that for the first time, organizations of all sorts can tap the deep tacit knowledge that their entire workforces (and, particularly in the case of crisis situations that thrust strangers into leadership role outsiders in some cases) have accumulated over time.

The data provides the real-time information. The collaborative tools provide the means to fully explore and integrate that information. Together, they create the opportunity to blast past practices to smithereens, improving data analysis and decision-making throughout society. When we do that, we can do things more quickly, integrate more perspectives, and adapt more rapidly than ever before. There has simply never been this kind of power and insight before.

As we will see in the following chapters, every aspect of human organizations and the quality of our lives will be transformed as a result.

DISTRICT OF COLUMBIA 2.0

THE PROTOTYPE INTEGRATED DATA-CENTRIC ORGANIZATION

Perhaps we should thank Mayor Marion Barry.

He left office as mayor of the District of Columbia in 1999, but the aura of corruption and mismanagement that developed during his administrations continues to cast a shadow over D.C.'s government, forcing his successors to put extra emphasis on transparency and reform to restore public faith.

When Adrian Fenty assumed the office of mayor in 2007, he brought in a group of bright young reformers including Vivek Kundra as the District's chief technology officer. He was charged with overseeing the 600-person Office of the Chief Technologist (OCTO), the agency that oversees IT spending and is charged with implementing IT projects throughout city government.

In the less than two years before he became the United States' first CIO, Kundra pioneered many of the specific data liberation practices that he has since implemented nationally. Equally important, but less reported, he began to use these same tools internally to help the District's workforce become more efficient and creative.[133]

What reformers like Kundra, Fenty, former D.C. Public Schools Chancellor Michelle A. Rhee, and others accomplished[134] was, to my knowledge the best model to date of a truly data-centric organization, and thus provides a lot of how-to information for other government agencies or businesses that want to become data-centric. Thus, it deserves a review in its own right as well as because it previews much of what Kundra will do in his current role, such as instituting the Data.gov site and creating the IT Dashboard to publicly show IT programs' progress or lack thereof.[135]

Vivek Kundra is much more than the technocratic stereotype of a CIO. He has a burning passion to make technology the means for achieving good government and to spread what he called "Participatory Democracy."[136] In fact, when interviewing for the post, he told Mayor Fenty he was only interested if he could have a mandate to "launch a technological revolution in government to make it better serve the people."[137]

Kundra, who was thirty-one at the time of his appointment, had seen the effects of bad government close hand while a boy in Tanzania. Since coming to the US at age thirteen, he developed a passion for US democracy (have you ever heard of anyone else who chose to be married at the US Constitution Center in Philadelphia?) that may be hard for more blasé native-born citizens to understand. Most important, he has translated that passion for democracy and good government into tangible, creative reforms.

VISION OF THE DIGITAL PUBLIC SQUARE

While working for Arlington County in Virginia, Kundra's office was in a municipal square, where residents frequently came together (if not necessarily really interacting) while renewing drivers licenses, attending public meetings, or shopping at the farmers' market. That reminded Kundra of ancient Athens, where residents attended to both commerce and their pioneering form of direct democracy in the *agora*, or public square. Kundra saw an opportunity to recreate the phenomenon of direct participation in government through what he calls the digital public square using Web 2.0 technologies such as YouTube and wikis. The concept informed all of his reform efforts. As he wrote:

❝ *Technological advances now allow people from around the world unfettered access to their government. Through these advances, constituents can hold their government accountable from the privacy of their own homes. The District of Columbia is bringing people closer to government through collaborative technologies like wikis, data feeds, videos and dashboards. We're throwing open D.C.'s warehouse of public data so that everyone—constituents, policymakers, and businesses—can meet in a new digital public square....We are ushering in a new age of participatory democracy, one in which citizens are in the driver's seat when they interact with government. Accessibility has never been greater, and this is just the beginning."* [138]

That vision guided Kundra's work for the District of Columbia. The result was a continuous data loop in which data was:

→ Collected in databases and warehouses.

→ Structured, so that it could easily be queried and seamlessly shared between various systems.

→ Distributed through automatic syndication so that it was available when and where it is needed, frequently on a real-time basis.

→ Made available to all workers who needed it, in forms they could use to manage their work and collaborate with others. [139]

→ Made available externally so that watchdog groups could analyze it, as a means to restore public confidence in government's integrity.

→ Made available externally in forms that enabled civic groups, entrepreneurs and individuals to become "co-creators" with government, integrating into applications, services, and even businesses that will improve civic life, individuals' lives, and create value and revenues.

AS IT STRATEGY EVOLVED, DATA REMAINED THE CORE

During Kundra's tenure, liberating data was at the heart of everything done by OCTO. At its core was the Citywide Data Warehouse, a growing catalogue of data feeds on all aspects of District Columbia government. The site emphasized it focused on "real-time operational data from multiple agencies and sources that enables decision support and government transparency."[140] Without it, none of these reforms and innovations would have been possible.

As of Kundra's departure to become the US chief information officer, the District was releasing more than 250 distinct data feeds, from juvenile arrest records to registered property.

DCSTAT PROGRAM

In fact, the District's leadership in smart use of structured data had begun even before Kundra arrived.

The District's structured data programs began when Kundra's predecessor, Suzanne Thomas, and her boss, city administrator Robert Bobb, launched the DCStat program. That in turn was inspired by the award-winning CityStat program that Martin O'Malley started when he was mayor of Baltimore (and later became the basis of StateStat when he was elected governor of Maryland). In all three programs, the emphasis was on providing objective analytical tools to help measure whether agencies were really performing.

"REAL DATA DOESN'T OCCUR VERTICALLY"

From the beginning, DCStat program director Dan Thomas emphasized structured data that hadn't been edited and therefore compromised, by officials. As Peck told data evangelist Jon Udell in a 2006 interview:

" Historically, information about the efficiency and the level of services across an enterprise, a municipal enterprise, has been vertically available function by function, agency by agency. But that kind of data isn't real data, because real data doesn't occur vertically. Real data occurs horizontally. If as a citizen, for example, the things most interesting to you, that you are most focused on are, am I getting the services I am paying for? Am I safe? Are my children well educated? The answers to those questions don't come from any particular vertical agency. The answers to those questions come horizontally in an integrated way across a number of agencies, each of whom provides a part of the answer to that question .....And if those things are not here, how does my city go about making sure that I am on the road to getting them? Those are all happening horizontally."[141]

THE ALPHABET SOUP OF DEMOCRATIZED DATA

Under Mayor Fenty, DC Stat evolved into the Citywide Data Warehouse (CDW).

It was closely linked to his version of CityStat, CAPStat, used specifically as a way to use data to improve agency performance.[142] CapStat data was used both on a continuing basis to improve daily operations and to drive "CAPStat accountability sessions." Those were weekly one-hour meetings in which the mayor and city administrator met with all of the city officials responsible for a given issue, to evaluate the relevant statistics and plan ways to improve performance.

Dan Thomas, who directed the DCStat program under Peck, explained in the 2006 interview with Udell that OCTO had capitalized from the beginning of DCStat on one of the most important aspects of structured data feeds: how the same data can be made valuable to a wide range of potential users by presenting it using a variety of different applications, each tailored to the information needs of a different audience.[143]

Because the data was all structured by use of XML tags, it became more versatile, because each of these "views" can emphasize different aspects of the data, while the data's integrity is preserved through the tags and metadata.

In the same interview, Peck illustrated how access to data across traditional agency boundaries let District of Columbia agencies analyze issues in fundamentally different ways that could put issues such a violent crime in perspective and bring resources beyond the traditional ones of additional police to bear on fighting crime:

> **"** *Why are things happening?....We and the police certainly understood that if there are crack houses, if there are abandoned autos, if there are nuisance properties, if there are poor school test scores, if there are high unemployment rates, that all of those things together not only positively contribute to crime but if you remove them all, have a negative effect on crime."*

During Peck's years as CTO the District of Columbia reduced crime by 23% in its fourteen worst hotspots, partially by being able to gather and distribute information in those areas on a real-time basis and partially due to the "HotSpot" initiative that focused various departments' resources on the highest-crime areas.[145]

Kundra built on Peck's foundation with additional emphasis on data-in data-out streams, giving the public access to the same data city agencies work with. When possible, he released the data on a real-time basis.

As Kundra says, not fudging the numbers is critical: "This is the data your government is using to make public policy decisions, so let's be honest, not try to clean it."[146] Kundra likes to compare the potential for innovation when everyone has equal access to structured information to both the GPS explosion since 2000 and the public Human Genome Project. Because the data about all publicly available, nucleotide sequences and their protein translations are stored in the open-access GenBank, there are now hundreds of drugs in the approval pipeline because of the free access to the information.

Kundra was adamant that data had to be the basis for all OCTO management decisions because it removes the subjective and gives an objective means to compare projects and their success.

Kundra likes to think of individual data feeds as the "alphabet" of a liberating data program, and that maximizing the feeds' usability requires a careful strategy of not presupposing how potential users will handle them, especially not prejudging what combinations of data will be most useful. In a quote harkening back to the Luther analogy in Chapter 1, he said:

> ❝ *The building blocks of language aren't sentences, they are the letters of the alphabet. Just think of all you can do with just twenty-six of them. People can apply their own creativity, driven by their own information needs, to build words, sentences and books. That's how we view our data feeds: present them in the most granular form and then let the users, from police to neighborhood residents, decide how to combine them. That way, the potential combinations are limit-less.*"[147]

SYSTEMATICALLY BUILDING DATA STREAMS

Kundra created a team that met and negotiated with agencies, signed a memorandum of understanding that mandated their data be shared publicly with minimum alteration, and outlined steps the agencies would take to maintain the data warehouse. Because Kundra didn't want to discourage structuring data and adding feeds, they tried to avoid creating new systems on top of existing ones. The team capitalized on XML's ability to work with a wide range of legacy systems rather than forcing them to launch a costly and time-consuming process of converting to a uniform system.[148] The OCTO staff also worked with the agencies to brainstorm all the end-to-end digital processes they could build.

To prioritize their work, the OCTO data analysis staff graphed potential feeds on a chart where the x axis is velocity: how quickly the feed can be created and shared, and the y axis is complexity: how difficult the project would be. They tried to strike a balance between some data that scored highly on each of the axes, with particular emphasis on some that might be complex but applied to overriding public policy issues, such as improving the public schools.

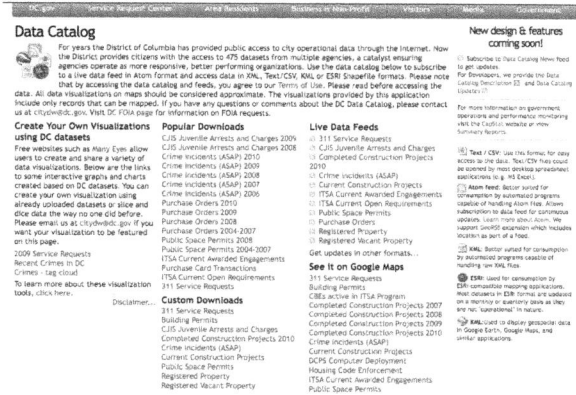

FIGURE 4-1: D.C. CITYWIDE DATA WAREHOUSE
Source: D.C. OCTO

Both to simplify adding additional feeds and to build a culture in which everyone automatically thinks of data feeds from the beginning of a project, Kundra eventually required that any new data project "bake in" relevant feeds, since doing it on the front end is simpler than having to add it later.[149]

KUNDRA'S STRATEGY

Kundra said that his OCTO strategy was common-sense based. "I try to draw lessons from the way I use technology to simplify my own life, and to ask simple questions about how government can serve the people more effectively."

During his confirmation hearing, he said that he would use a three-part strategy to improve OCTO's performance:

➜ Emphasize use of disruptive technologies.

➜ Use a business intelligence platform to drive decisions.

➜ Rethink how government delivers services.[150]

He followed through on each of these priorities.

DISRUPTIVE TECHNOLOGIES

Picking up on Clayton Christensen's *The Innovator's Dilemma*, Kundra emphasized perhaps the most disruptive technologies of recent years: the shift toward "cloud computing," where software is hosted by a vendor rather than being installed on each computer, and toward open standards, not only using XML, but also open-standard applications. For example, he contracted for 38,000 seats of Google Apps, the suite of applications that Google hosts itself in a "cloud," so they don't have to be installed and maintained. He also emphasized using consumer technology such as smartphones and Gmail.[151]

THE OCTO STOCK EXCHANGE

For the Business Intelligence (BI) component of his strategy, Kundra could have bought a conventional, pricey, and proprietary application. It would typically have given him a dashboard to analyze historical, current, and future views of various parts of OCTO's operations based on Citywide Data Warehouse data. It probably would have allowed him and the OCTO staff to do reports, benchmarking, predictions, and "scorecards."

However, he instead pursued a decidedly unconventional BI strategy, based on an "a-ha moment".

Kundra was frustrated that he couldn't find an easy way to compare various OCTO initiatives to each other on a consistent, quantifiable basis, and, particularly, how to compare their ROI.

One day it occurred to him that people who are weighing which stocks to buy can compare many more alternatives on an objective basis, and they can do this because of stock markets and commonly used performance indices. As he explained it in a profile when he was the youngest person selected for *InfoWorld*'s 25 CTOs of 2008:

> **❝** *'In my private life, I am in real time on my smartphone checking out the status of my stocks and the management team, so why can't I do that in the D.C. government?' he asked himself one day. That's when it hit him: Manage IT as if it were a portfolio of stocks, with each project being a 'company,' its team being the management, its schedule and financial management being the quarterly reports, and the customer satisfaction to deliverables being the market reaction."*

Kundra hired a team of analysts to track projects the way stock analysts would.[152]

After the stock exchange model was adopted, visitors to the Office of the Chief Technology Officer found their eyes riveted on the large, open room on the right: the IT stock exchange room. Instead of a typical governmental cube farm, small clusters of open cubes were scattered around the floor, while the walls are dominated by an array of large smart screens.

On each of the displays, five or six striking graphics, part of an application built in-house on an open-source platform, showed individual technology projects' current status, including indicators such as cost, project milestones, and a "happiness" index that quantifies the level of satisfaction with the project on the part of those who would eventually use it. It's a prime example of the value of data visualization that was explored in Chapter 3: statistics that might have little meaning if they were simply presented in row upon row, but rivet your attention when portrayed visually.

Kundra didn't just apply the stock market model to tracking projects on a daily basis.

To oversee major projects from start to finish he created IT investment boards composed of officials from his office, the CFO's office, and the agencies for which the projects were being created. They evaluated the "portfolio" at least quarterly on cost, time, and value. Project teams were told that at the end of each quarter, "under-performing" stocks (i.e., projects that consistently rank below the 70% cutoff level) would be "sold," i.e., the projects terminated and the money was redeployed for other projects. The program's actual impact was limited; although it may well have motivated other teams to work harder to avoid being "sold," only one project was actually terminated by Kundra, an intranet portal that cost $4 million without ever resulting in a usable product.[153]

While the stock market approach may seem harsh (and Kundra acknowledged that he "ruthlessly" made data the means for evaluating results), in fact it is more equitable than the more traditional practice, whether in government or corporations, of subjectively evaluating progress toward completing a project. As Kundra told *InfoWorld*:

> ❝ *I wanted a more data-driven model; after all, the data is the data. If you're over budget for two or three quarters, you can't avoid being exposed....People don't make tough decisions easily, so you have to show them the data. [As government leaders,] it's our duty to make sure they're periodically assessing progress against them subjectively. Not failing....Objective measurements make that assessment easier.*❞[154]

Because the data was freely available to all of the OCTO employees 24/7, and because it was based on objective criteria, those who were working on a project that was lagging compared to other projects knew well before the quarter was over that their project—and they—were in danger and had to take substantive, quantifiable actions that would translate to higher ranking on all of the evaluation criteria, and, in particular, the "happiness" index.

Thus, while it may seem harsh, the approach was likely to result in a more equitable and merit-based workplace. Kundra has continued this approach on the federal level with "IT Dashboards" that he has imposed on major IT projects. Each tracks the progress (or lack thereof) of a given project, and can be the basis for discontinuing a project that fails to make adequate progress toward completion and effectiveness.

RETHINK HOW GOVERNMENT DELIVERS SERVICES

The third component of Kundra's strategy at OCTO was to rethink how government delivers services. It is perhaps that aspect of OCTO's operations that was most revolutionary again, made possible by liberating data.

First, he was adamant about getting municipal workers the real-time, location-based data they needed to do their jobs more efficiently and collaboratively.

Kundra didn't buy the vision that advanced technology and particularly emphasis to actionable data should be the province of senior management, while rank-and-file workers muddled through as they always have.

By contrast, he emphasized that "every worker must be a knowledge worker," with access to the real-time information needed to do his or her job more efficiently.

A good example of the new attitude in practice was a high-visibility initiative early in 2008 to get 6,300 new computers into the Washington School system, a priority of School Chancellor Rhee.

An earlier plan, before OCTO assumed responsibility for the schools' IT, was estimated to take a year for procurement and installation of the computers. Using OCTO's GIS resources, the IT ServUS PC team was able to plan the most efficient routes through the city to install and program the computers. As a result, they were able to cut the installation process to only seven weeks.[155]

In another example, in which access to real-time, location-based information may literally be a matter of life-or-death, D.C. installed 2,600 laptops in police cruisers, and tied them to the Global Positioning System and to mobile Internet connections. That let dispatchers see, in real-time, where the closest cruiser was to a 911 caller, and allowed real-time management of police resources.

In the summer of 2008 OCTO introduced a new intranet that gave individual workers the data they needed to do their work more efficiently, typically presented using data visualization tools that made them more easily understood. [156]

The workers also had access to tools that foster collaboration, such as Google apps, microblogging, and the DCpedia wiki for sharing information. As a result, long-standing agency silos crumbled and there was more and more collaboration. Interestingly, once they could collaborate more easily, rank-and-file workers began to hold each other accountable. (The intense preparations and inflexible deadlines required for President Obama's inauguration particularly encouraged collaboration and peer pressure to complete on time.)[157]

"CONTEXT IS KING"

It's hard to over-emphasize how important the ability to take the exact same structured data and use it in multiple ways became to OCTO's liberating data strategy.

Because the data streams, once created, could be made accessible anywhere, Kunda could deliver on another of his pet priorities, taking government services to the places where people can easily access them, rather than making the people come to D.C. offices during business hours. Because the incremental cost of finding another way to use them was very small, that also further amortized the original cost of creating the data streams.

One of the most novel applications of what Kundra called his "context is king" approach was a new program that let D.C. residents who are doing simple renovations apply for their building permits guess where? Not at the permitting office, but at Home Depot, where they were going anyway to buy the supplies! As a bonus, the permitting isn't limited to the office's 8:30 AM to 5:00 PM schedule, but anytime Home Depot is open.[158]

Similarly, a service to help college students deal with illegal practices by landlords could be accessed at the logical place to reach this audience, a Facebook group (those paying parking fines could also do so on another District Facebook page).

Kundra said he was just being realistic, bringing services to the places on the Web that people are most likely to congregate, rather than forcing them to come to the DC.gov site and within their office schedules. "After all, we're here to serve them."[159]

START SMALL, THEN SCALE

The school computers program was very large and highly visible. Given his druthers, Kundra preferred to start with small demonstration programs, work the kinks out, then scale up (or, using the stock market model, quickly pull the plug before expenses mounted). He modeled his OCTO Labs on the Google Labs model, doing small-scale implementations, and then scaling it up if it worked. "It's very much based on a venture capital model. Some of these ideas will fail," he said. "But the beauty of it is you've made a modest investment, and if it scales, you'll create enough value that the funding will come because the agencies want to pay for it."[160]

INTEGRATING CHANGE: REVOLUTIONIZING PROCUREMENT

Perhaps none of Kundra's innovations integrated so many aspects of his thinking as the way he revolutionized the District's procurement process. When you think about it, no matter what the organization governmental or corporate, there's nothing that is normally so bureaucratic and opaque, two factors that significantly increase the chance of corruption and inefficiency, and reduce public access to the facts.

Building on reforms that he began while serving as Virginia governor Tim Kaine's assistant secretary of commerce and technology, Kundra transformed D.C. IT procurement into a Web 2.0-based process that dramatically reduced costs to taxpayers, made it more fair for all participants, and made it easier for watchdog groups, the media, and taxpayers to monitor.

Almost every aspect of procurement was radically altered from the normal process:

➔ For a project to build a new evidence warehouse for the police and to develop better ways to manage evidence, OCTO created a wiki and YouTube videos so participants could share information and ideas.

➔ Bidders conferences were broadcast on YouTube.

➔ Because the District standardized on the cloud-based Google Apps suite, which facilitates online collaboration, the process of writing procurement documents was faster.[161]

The benefits were impressive:

➔ All bidders gained equal access to information throughout the process, making it both more fair and reducing the chances of legal challenges (ignorance is no defense!). A much broader range of potential vendors could participate, which increased competition and drove down prices.

➔ The collaborative process using the wiki allowed more interested parties to participate, and increased the chances that potential issues that might otherwise have gone overlooked would not only surface, but also be discussed fully and solved.

➔ Public confidence in the process was increased because of the transparency (For example, all of the bids for a given contract are attached as pdf files on the wiki).

TRANSPARENCY

Mayor Fenty launched a comprehensive transparency initiative in every aspect of municipal operations, with particular emphasis on spending. Building on the procurement reforms, Kundra planned to make the District of Columbia's spending and procurement as transparent as possible. During 2008, one of the feeds added to the Citywide Data Warehouse was the one for purchase orders greater than $2,500, and the agency also began to publish all recent credit card transactions.

THE BLEEDING EDGE: APPS FOR DEMOCRACY

Most of the benefits that the District of Columbia achieved through its liberating data program were incremental, largely due to the increased efficiency of better coordination; giving workers the information they need, when and where they need it, to manage their work more efficiently; and allowing innovative ways of delivering existing services.

Where the program really broke new ground was the month-long Apps for Democracy contest that Kundra ran during October, 2008 that was mentioned briefly in Chapter 1.

On September 11, 2008 Kundra invited in Peter Corbett, a passionate leader of the growing community of young, non-defense-establishment D.C. technologists, and CEO of iStrategy Labs, to discuss how to best capitalize on the D.C. Citywide Data Warehouse.

Corbett told Kundra that he could go the traditional multi-year, big budget procurement route that would be costly and might not work, or "Put the data in the hands of the people, and give them cash prizes and recognition for their efforts". Two days later, Corbett submitted a proposal, and by October 15th, OCTO launched its competition, Apps for Democracy, focused on how to use public data to serve the public interest.

Kundra and Corbett decided to up the ante: entrants in the D.C. contest would have to submit not ideas on how to use data, but full-fledged applications that would be ready to go at the end of the month-long contest.

For those used to complicated governmental procurement requests for proposals, the rules were laughably simple:

→ Use one or more of the D.C. Citywide Data Warehouse feeds.

→ Provide a public benefit such as visualization, or data analysis.

→ Use open source code so that others could copy and/or improve on the application.

CITIZENS AS CO-CREATORS OF GOVERNMENT

Kundra's vision for the competition was that it would go far beyond any of his prior innovations toward realizing the digital public square, because the public would actually be full partners. "We are ushering in a new age of participatory democracy," he said, "One in which technology is developed by the people for the people. In the nation's capital we are treating citizens not as subjects, but as co-creators of government."[163]

Kundra also had another goal in mind: creating "buzz" in technology circles that Washington is a neat place to live and work, and there is more going on than creating massive closed systems for the Pentagon.

The contest ran slightly under a month, and by the deadline, forty-seven very different applications were posted on the website, ready for use by the public.

The entries were judged on:

→ Usefulness to the citizens, visitors and the government.

→ Appeal from a usability perspective.

→ Inventive and original nature of the application.

→ Potential to be useful for other governments.

One of the award winners significantly bolstered Fenty and Kundra's efforts to make D.C. government more accountable and transparent. The "We the People" wiki was "a peer-led community reference website that you can edit based on Washington, D.C. public data. We the People empowers all of us to make D.C. a more responsive community where all voices are heard and each of us can make a difference". Then there was the very practical "Peoples' Choice" winner, the Carpool Mashup Maker to help D.C. residents create carpools.

One entrant, Adam Boalt of Boalt Interactive, applied some of the same thinking Kundra does when he tries to apply his personal life to meeting technology needs. Boalt, who had scored big as an entrepreneur during the previous year with his highly successful RushMyPassport.com service, had recently moved to D.C. with his girlfriend. They were avid walkers, and also interested in D.C. history, but couldn't find "an all-encompassing source." So he created an application for iPhones called DC Historic Tours, which combines Flickr photos and Wikipedia entries to create walking tours based on the individual's specific interests, rather than the standard one-size-fits-all map tours. Because users can add additional content, crowdsourcing will only make it more robust over time.

Not only are the applications helping citizens and tourists, but D.C. agencies have closely reviewed them, and several agencies now routinely monitor the applications for helpful information that they can't glean from their existing official ones.

From the results, it would appear Kundra was successful both on turning the citizenry into co-creators of government services and in creating "buzz".

And, it might be added, he was also creating a powerful model for other organizations of any kind at a time when the economy was in disarray and everyone's budgets were being cut drastically: turn your customers into active partners at a fraction of the normal program cost. As we will see in the next chapter, that's exactly what other government agencies are doing worldwide, directly inspired by Apps for Democracy.

Peter Corbett informally calculated a 4000% return on investment on the $50,000 expenditure ($20,000 in prizes, and $30,000 in administrative expenses), not to mention the fact that if Kundra had gone a conventional route, issuing a request for proposals, and used even his greatly-improved procurement process, he probably would have still been in the early stages of designing the RFP on the day when Mayor Fenty instead announced the winners.

The mayor said that within the month forty-seven workable applications were actually available for use by DC residents and workers, compared to an estimated one to two years development time with a conventional procurement approach.

A conventional approach would not have yielded anywhere near as many usable applications. It would be unrealistic to think that any centralized technical organization such as OCTO, no matter how creative, would have been able to visualize some of these applications in order to request their development. It is no criticism of any government worker, to say that they would have been unlikely to think of creating an application to track road-kill, one component of one of the winners, or, unless they were avid riders, that they'd dream up the one for bike lanes.

Apps for Democracy received a wide range of favorable publicity worldwide.

Blogger Matthew Burton said the timing of the competition was right, especially given the state of the economy, because officials "can use their budget shortfall as an opportunity to create a better system. They can starve their slow-moving, wasteful systems, or they can try newly evolved, more efficient systems. Compared to a government contractor, independent web developers are cheap–even free, sometimes....If a crisis is the best time for bold ideas, then Apps for Democracy couldn't have come at a better time".[164]

EQUALLY APPLICABLE TO BUSINESS

Vivek Kundra is adamant: the liberating data approach is equally important and relevant to the private sector. In fact, while at OCTO he entertained a stream of venture capitalists and companies interested in his approach's relevance to the corporate world.

A MODEL, NOT A MOLD

Vivek Kundra left OCTO too soon to be able to create a comprehensive, integrated data-centric organization. In particular, internal use of real-time data to help workers make better decisions and collaborate across agency boundaries fell far short of his vision of a workforce in which "every worker is a knowledge worker."

However, the agency definitely exhibited many of the attributes of the data-centric organization of the future:

> ➔ Data was structured whenever possible, so that it had context and meaning that would be sustained no matter how it was used.

> ➔ The presumption was data should be shared, not hoarded. Exceptions to

that rule had to be justified, not just be a blanket prohibition.

➜ Data was used to objectify evaluation of projects in the stock market system, and to give everyone involved real-time information needed to meet evaluation criteria.

➜ Data was delivered to users, as in the case of the new remote home improvement permitting system, instead of forcing them to adapt to bureaucratic routine or beg through a Freedom of Information Act request.

➜ Unprecedented transparency regarding government spending was used to restore public confidence in governmental integrity.

➜ At least some workers got real-time access to data to help them make better decisions and collaborate with others.

➜ OCTO partnered with the user community to create new services through the Apps for Democracy competition. Government provided the necessary data, and the user provided the creative new uses.

➜ Open-source applications and allowing free access to Apps for Democracy code both cut operating costs and made it simpler for other governmental and business organizations to adopt and adapt DC's solutions. That dramatically reduces the adoption curve and spreads the benefits of data liberation.

As inspiring as OCTO under Vivek Kundra may have been, it by no means should be seen as *the* model for a data-centric organization, because open data and a spirit of collaboration opens an infinite number of possible ways of achieving the data-centric goal.

In fact, as we will see in the next chapter, perhaps tiny (6,000 residents) Manor, Texas is the most inspiring model of all for a data-centric organization, because it accomplished astonishing results on a $100,000 IT budget.

GOVERNMENT BLAZES THE TRAIL

Government accountability and transparency pioneer Gary Bass remembers when the US government started experimenting with direct release of data to citizens. It was in 1989, when the Toxic Release Inventory (TRI) was launched, to inform the public about volumes of hazardous materials being released in their neighborhoods.

The experimenting wasn't pretty.

Bass, founder and director of the governmental watchdog and transparency group OMB Watch, recalls meeting at EPA, when the agency had "no clue how to proceed. They were required to release the information through 'computer available means at reasonable reimbursement rates.' It was mind boggling to EPA: this program had enormous policy implications and they didn't know what to do."[165]

EPA eventually worked with the National Library of Medicine to administer the program. The NLM put the information up, and it used proprietary software that cost too much. Users had to pay per minute for dial-up access.

A less than auspicious beginning!

Today, by contrast, a convergence of politics and unprecedented events has brought us to a point where liberating governmental data has become an (hopefully) unstoppable global phenomenon.

LIBERATING DATA KEY TO ACHIEVING POLICY GOALS

Done creatively, liberating government data can simultaneously achieve a wide range of goals that have emerged in recent years, especially since the global recession began in 2008. They have both increased the need for government services while simultaneously reducing public confidence in government's ability to deliver them and to do so economically. Those goals include:

➜ Speed service delivery, especially executing economic recovery programs.

➜ Cut operating costs by streamlining services and eliminating redundancy.

➜ Improve service by being able to target them more precisely and help government workers make better decisions.

➜ Reduce regulatory costs for companies.

➜ Improve quality of regulation and consumer protection.

➜ Stimulate economic development through valuable real-time data that can be mashed up with other data.

Remember how tagged data can flow anywhere that the same tags are inserted? It is that factor that can facilitate these multiple improvements. We no longer must choose between these worthwhile goals. The same data can be put to work simultaneously addressing all of these needs.

That means that not only can the data flow back to the public (whose lives, purchases and work were, after all, the ultimate source of that data), but it can also flow seamlessly within all branches of government, leading to better decision-making because personnel will have the information they need to do their work, plus streamlining and cost reductions because various programs and agencies that need to work with the same data can now do so simultaneously and even cooperatively.

While we're at it, let's spread the wealth around.

Literally. As with the vast and growing array worldwide of location-based services

(LBS) that were enabled by the US government's release of real-time geo-spatial GPS information, the increased amount of data (especially the real-time variety) that governments now release for free will doubtlessly lead to additional entrepreneurial companies capitalizing on them.

Government often is a laggard when it comes to technology innovation, but when it comes to real-time access to data, the situation is much more like the birth of the Internet or the space race: governments all over the world are far ahead of the private sector, and indeed blazing the trail. Even better, they are doing so in a spirit of collaboration and using open source tools that make it easy for latecomers and those with fewer financial resources to not only copy the early adopters, but to often offer their own refinements to services that benefit everyone.

Accordingly, I will go into more detail about the widely varied governmental open data initiatives rather than the handful of ones by the private sector, to inspire (hopefully) the business community to follow suit.

FROM THE OUTSIDE IN: THE TRANSPARENCY PIONEERS

FCC Chief Data Officer Greg Ellin recalls the 1990s as, at best, a time of behind-the-scenes advances for the concept of transparency. "People who are idealists, interested in public interest, got diverted in the 1990s to inventing the various online tools that would make transparency programs feasible, such as wikis and XML tag systems", He says it took activists a while to begin applying these tools to transparency, but when that did happen, it was dramatically different from the old "disclosure" initiatives from before watchdog groups had easy access to the Web: "There's something different about Internet transparency: releasing this information on the Internet means never having to ask for permission."[166]

MYSOCIETY.ORG

British activist Tom Steinberg, founder of MySociety.org, was among the pioneers in the 1990s. The group has been around long enough that one of its sites tellingly was originally titled FaxYourMP. It has two missions: building web sites that produce simple, tangible benefits in civic and community aspects of their lives; and teaching government, by demonstrating, how to use the Web to improve people's lives.[167]

MySociety.org is perhaps best known for its FixMyStreets site,[168] a pioneer in what has been called "sousveillance". If your French is a little rusty, "sous"means "under", so sousveillance is the mirror image of surveillance: we all know government is watching us, through surveillance cameras, etc., but sousveillance flips the coin so that members of the public can hold government accountable for what it is or isn't doing.[169]

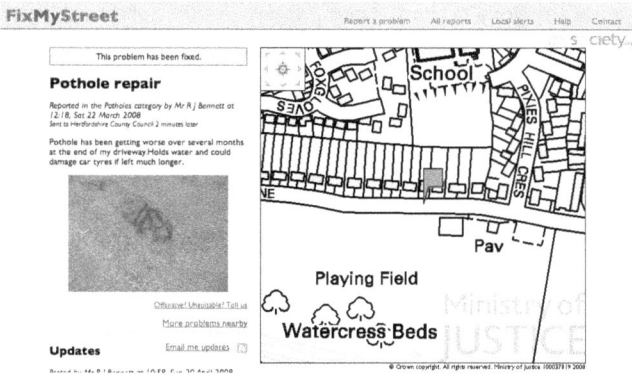

ILLUSTRATION 5-1: FIXMYSTREET
source: FixMyStreet.org

It couldn't be simpler: "Enter your postcode, stick a pin in the map, type in your problem and zoom! Off it goes to the council". FixMyStreet also lets citizens monitor and analyze these problems, through tools such as RSS feeds that will alert you when problems are reported within a certain radius of your home that you choose.[170]

Perhaps most important in terms of its overall effectiveness, and setting the expectations for the collaborative spirit behind many governmental transparency efforts, FixMyStreet was built on open source code, "for people who want to hack versions in other countries". As we will see throughout the innovations in government and civic transparency and open data sites, groups and government agencies that are not transparency pioneers can quickly establish credible services by making simple changes to these early examples, speeding the movement's spread. Indeed, one of the most popular Gov. 2.0 apps in the United States, SeeClickFix, was directly inspired by FixMyStreet.[171]

MySociety also has a variety of sites that reflect a major theme of transparency efforts worldwide: holding elected officials accountable by documenting their actions and making it easier to interact with them. For example, WritetoThem.com makes it easy to write your elected officials: simply enter your postcode and the information on how to contact your officials automatically pops up. HearFromYourMP makes it easy for Members of Parliament (MPs) to send out bulletins to constituents, and TheyWorkForYou is a comprehensive site documenting MPs' voting records, speeches, etc. [172]

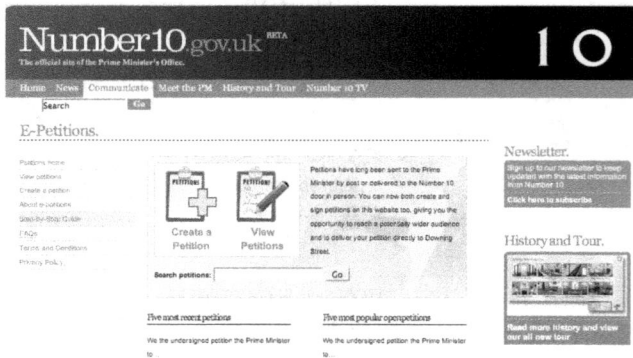

ILLUSTRATION 5-2 NUMBER 10.GOV.UK E-PETITIONS SITE
source: MySociety

MySociety has earned such a reputation that it was given a contract by the prime minister's office in 2006 to design the official No. 10 Petitions Website so that citizens could petition the PM online. Before the site was suspended in 2011 as another government site assumed the role, it was reportedly the world's largest non-partisan democracy site (in terms of volume of users), with more than twelve million signatures. MySociety insisted on a number of conditions before beginning the

DATA DYNAMITE: How Liberating Information Will Transform Our World

project that should be models for other sites, including using open-source code, and retaining users' private data on mySociety's servers, not the government's.[173]

Tom Steinberg's passion for his work is obvious. He's blunt about the benefits of transparency and public access to data: "All the services that government and other sectors provide can be improved through smart use of public data to increase transparency, accountability and simple comprehensibility".[174]

"SUNLIGHT IS THE MOST POWERFUL OF DISINFECTANTS"

Perhaps the closest parallel to mySociety in the US is the D.C.-based Sunlight Foundation. Founded in 2006, it takes its name from a saying of Justice Brandeis that "Sunlight is the most powerful of disinfectants"[175]

The non-partisan group's mission focuses totally on the Web to make information about Congress and the federal government accessible to the public, and in ways it's usable to bring about more governmental openness and accountability, based on "a fundamental belief that increased transparency will improve the conduct of Congress itself and the public's confidence in government."[176]

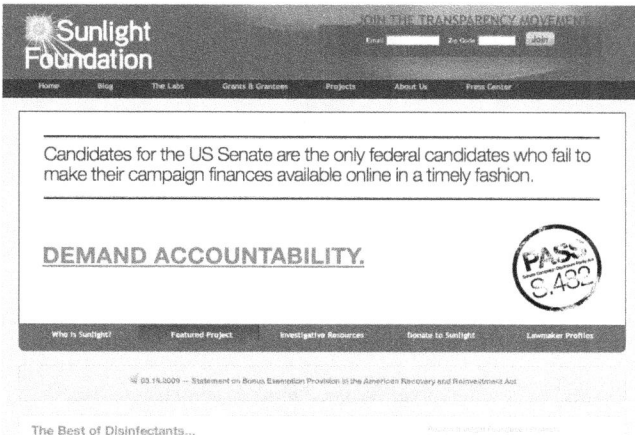

ILLUSTRATION 5-3 SUNLIGHT FOUNDATION HOMEPAGE
source: Sunlight Foundation

Sunlight is distinctive because it not only develops and maintains a wide range of websites around every aspect of government transparency and access to data (as of December, 2010 it had sixteen active projects underway), but it operates Sunlight Labs, an open-source development team that both creates technology for Sunlight projects and for spin-off projects.[177] It also provides seed money for start-up web-based transparency organizationSunlight's websites are all attractive, and it makes no bones about crisp design and easy-of-use data visualization tools being key elements in their strategy: "We spend a lot of time finding ways to make data useful to the general public. Staring at spreadsheets is boring and confusing. Data has to be presented in a way that is intriguing, visually appealing, and easy to understand."[178]

Sunlight's also very nimble. When it came to light that Congress passed the final, 1,100-page version of the American Recovery and Reinvestment Act of 2009 stimulus bill within thirteen hours of receiving the conference committee version, and without having fully read all of its provisions, Sunlight quickly started a Read the Bill petition, demanding that Congress make it a policy to post all legislation on line for seventy-two hours, no matter how crucial prompt action may be, so that members can read it and the public can also examine it and contact their elected officials about their concerns.[179]

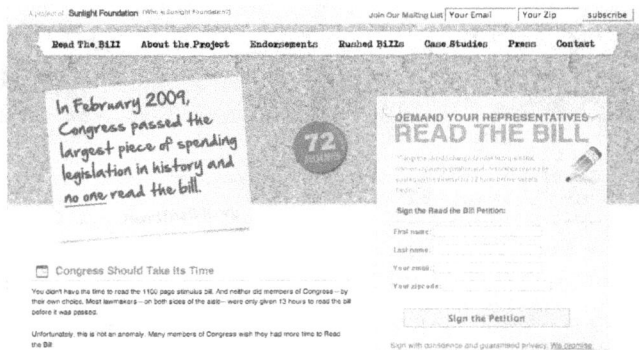

ILLUSTRATION 5-4 READ THE BILL
source: Sunlight Foundation

For all its emphasis on attractive visualizations, the Sunlight Foundation is more focused on the larger issue of assuring public access to data, and making sure that it is in a usable format, especially tagged with metadata that gives it meaning and context. As Executive Director Ellen Miller says, "The big thing is collecting the data. It's much simpler to take advantage of it."[180] Former Sunlight staffer Clay Johnson adds that "quality data is the easiest data,"[181] because it is so much harder to improve data quality once it has been collected and entered into an agency's system.

While the Sunlight Foundation may be the most prominent transparency and accountability group at this point, the field is rapidly expanding, particularly organizations on the state level with a libertarian and/or conservative slant, such as MaineOpenGov.org.

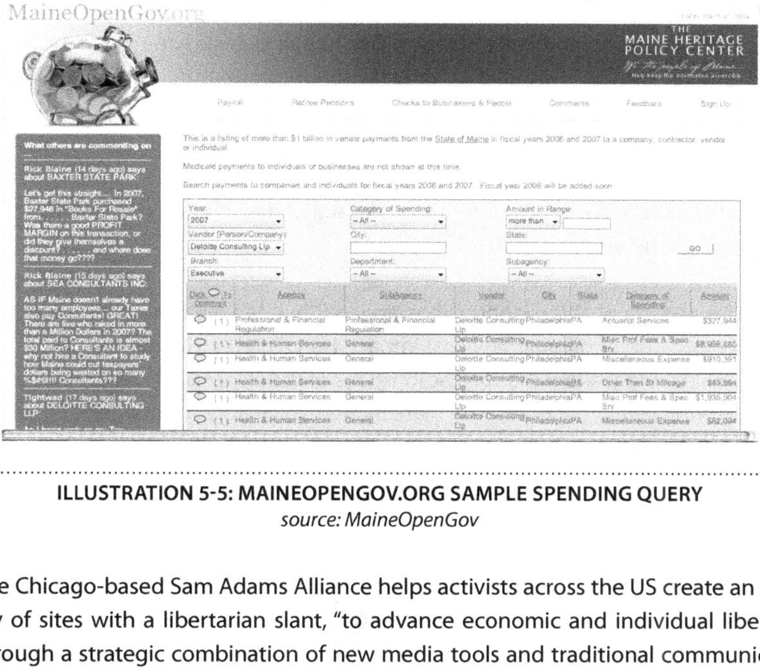

ILLUSTRATION 5-5: MAINEOPENGOV.ORG SAMPLE SPENDING QUERY
source: MaineOpenGov

The Chicago-based Sam Adams Alliance helps activists across the US create an array of sites with a libertarian slant, "to advance economic and individual liberty through a strategic combination of new media tools and traditional communications."[182]

Despite ideological differences, the various transparency and accountability sites frequently work for common goals such as free access to data and delaying legislative votes to allow more review.

INDIVIDUAL AND AD HOC PROJECTS

As impressive as the work by various formal organizations to promote transparency and accountability has been, the low barriers to entry as a result of open-source Web 2.0 technologies mean that some of the most interesting examples providing open access to government data and/or working with it have come from ad hoc efforts and/or individuals with a burning interest in a given issue.

RAMI TABELLO'S ILLEGALSIGNS.CA

A Toronto resident, Rami Tabello wants to rid his city of illegal billboards. As he says, wryly, "Everyone should have a hobby. Our hobby is destroying illegal billboards with the rule of law."[183] He has continually run into opposition from city officials, and in fact at one point City Clerk Ulli Watkiss tried to stop Tabello from filing Freedom of Information (FOI) requests, labeling them as "frivolous and vexatious."[184]

However, Tabello has forced the city to take action on billboards that are oversized and/or lack the proper permits.

His site was (as of this writing it has apparently been suspended) particular effective because of billboards' visual impact. He created a Google map of the city with pointers that show the specific locations of the illegal signs. As you'd imagine, people who lived near one of the markers were invariably curious enough to click on them. The popup shows a photo of the specific billboard and summarizes the legal issues involved.

ILLUSTRATION 5-6: ILLEGAL BILLBOARDS MAP
source: IllegalSigns.ca

City Councilor Howard Moscoe credited Tabello with using the site to win a court battle in February 2009 that required removal of a large number of billboards throughout Toronto. "The processes the city has set up have become very flabby," he said. "It's through agitation that we've been forced to be accountable."[185]

JACQUELINE DUPREE'S JDLAND

By contrast to Tabello's fights with City Hall, southeast Washington, D.C. resident Jacqueline Dupree subscribes to the growing number of automated feeds from D.C.'s Citywide Data Warehouse described in the prior chapter to power her award-winning JDLand site, chronicling development issues in the area near Washington Nationals Stadium.[186] In 2008 Dupree won the Knight-Batten Citizen Media Award for Innovation in Journalism. Judges said her site provided "an incredible wealth of information, especially impressive for a one-person effort."

Real-time D.C. downloads greatly facilitate the site's informativeness, making it a preview of the kind of hyper-local neighborhood journalism[187] now feasible since other municipalities are following D.C.'s lead with structured data feeds. If you decide to follow Dupree's lead, you will find it much easier than she did, both because of the ready availability of real-time data and because of the active global networks of individuals who are committed to "hyperlocal" news.

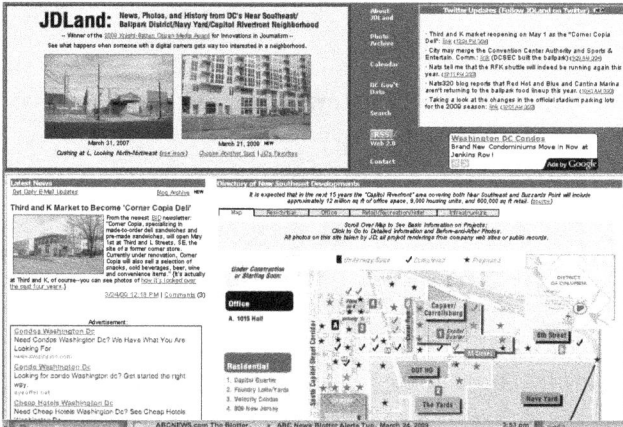

ILLUSTRATION 5-7: JDLAND SOUTHEAST WASHINGTON SITE
source: JDLand

CROWDSOURCING ANALYSIS: THE GONZALES CONTRO-VERSY

A totally different approach to transparency of government data and accountability arose spontaneously in 2007, when Talking Points Memo blogger Josh Marshall mobilized his readers to follow up when the first small story about the politically-motivated removal of US attorneys surfaced.

Marshall asked his readers to write if they had any information about US attorneys in other regions. Over several months, the TPM readers documented the full extent of the controversy, leading ultimately to Attorney General Alberto Gonzales's resignation. Equally important in terms of liberating data, once the Department of Justice released reams of documents about the controversy, the TPM readers volunteered to each analyze small chunks of the material, dramatically speeding up the analysis process (after all, sometimes in the past the most effective technique by a governmental agency to quiet a controversy would be to release such vast quantities of material that people would be overwhelmed!).[188]

Ultimately, TPM won the prestigious George Polk Award for Legal Reporting. While the citation only mentioned Marshall and two staffers, in reality it was the large number of reader/contributors dicing up the materials that made the report possible.[189]

Rep. John Culberson, R-TX, used the same approach to crowdsource analysis of the 2010 health care reform bill using the Sharedbook software.[190]

GOVERNMENT TAKES THE INITIATIVE

You will remember from Chapter 2 that the United States government took a critical step toward liberating data when it stopped distorting GPS data in 2000, leading to the explosion in location-based services built on that precise real-time geo-spatial information. One might have thought that instant success would have quickly led to widespread release of other data, but it did not.

DUTCH TAXONOMY PROJECT

Instead, the next major step in governmental data innovation came in 2004 when the Netherlands began to develop the "Dutch Taxonomy Project," which was detailed in Chapter 2. When formally launched in 2007, it proved to be a win-win solution, helping businesses and government alike.[191] Even better, the program demonstrated how easy it is, because of open, global standards to inspire virtuous imitations, such as the Standard Business Reporting system in Australia and pending ones in New Zealand and Singapore.

SHOW US A BETTER WAY

One of the more dramatic examples in the early stages of government data liberation initiatives came in the summer of 2008. UK cabinet officer minister Tom Watson's Task Force on the Power of Information ran a public contest with the delightfully un-bureaucratic name of "Show Us a Better Way" (when was the last time you ever heard a government official asking you to show them anything, let alone a better way?).[192]

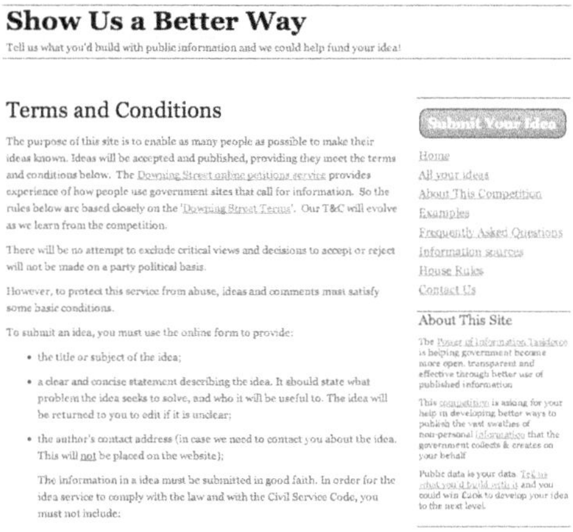

ILLUSTRATION 5-8: SHOW US A BETTER WAY COMPETITION
source: Task Force on the Power of Information

The description of the competition continued that same air of humility and apparently sincere desire to involve the public:

"Ever been frustrated that you can't find out something that ought to be easy to find? Ever been baffled by league tables or 'performance indicators'? Do you think that better use of public information could improve health, education, justice or society at large? The UK Government wants to hear your ideas for new products that could improve the way public information is communicated. The Power of Information Task force is running a competition on the Government's behalf, and we have a £20,000 prize fund.

"The government produces masses of information on what is happening around the UK. Information on crime, on health, on education. However, this information is often hidden away in obscure publications or odd corners of websites. Data tucked away like this isn't of use to the ultimate owner of that information YOU."[193]

Whoa! The government not only is asking for your ideas, but also willing to pay for them? You can imagine that caught the public's attention!

During the next two months, a wide range of people entered the competition. Some obviously had technical background in data analysis and programming. Others just had a problem that they thought might be fixed if government data were easily available.

The UK and its government were automatic winners: unlike traditional competitions, where entries are swallowed up and only the top winners are ever seen, all entries were posted on the contest website as soon as they were screened, so other people could examine them and perhaps submit a variation on the same theme. Meanwhile, government officials could gain ideas simply by monitoring the site: just because an entry wasn't an eventual winner didn't mean it might not have some merit.

The Task Force jury finally selected fourteen winners: five that the government committed to building, five existing ones they would support, and four early-stage ideas they would help develop further. [194]

Consistent with the decision to allow anyone to enter and not establish any qualifications, the winners ranged from rather sophisticated ones, such as the "Roadworks API," which would help build real-time construction information into other services; to rather elementary ones, such as the overall winner, a suggestion that the government create an application that would allow people to simply input their post code and find out what products could be recycled locally. [195]

LOOFINDER: TARGETED SERVICE THROUGH LIBERATING DATA

Cynics might scoff at one of the winners, LooFinder.[196] As with Stumble Safely, the D.C. Apps for Democracy winner described in Chapter 1, why should the government underwrite development of a service to help you find a public bathroom? To most of us, that might seem a little silly. However, if you are elderly, suffer from chronic incontinence or have small children, this could be a very important service.

It's unlikely that a government agency would have thought of such a service itself, but if government records this kind of data in its geo-spatial databases, and a citizen brings to its attention the need for such a service, shouldn't the government (or a public-minded programmer on the outside) oblige if the cost is low enough? A number of bathroom location sites have cropped up around the world since LooFinder.

As Prof. Nigel Shadbolt, an advisor to the UK government's transparency program, pointed out, the third-largest number of downloads of iPhone apps in the UK at one point was for "ASBOmeter," which mashes up what he referred to as a "dusty" data base compiled by the Home Office of what in the UK are referred to as "Anti-Social Behaviour" incidents to show the prevalence of these types of acts in a given neighborhood.[197] Former Prime Minister Gordon Brown even highlighted it in a speech as a prime example of the benefits of releasing government data for public use.[198]

It's almost magic: release data and you can almost be certain that someone with a passion for a given issue will find an imaginative way to use it.[199] That's no knock on government workers: just acknowledgment of the fact that when you open idea generation to everyone, you're more likely to find someone who will be highly motivated to use that data for a given issue!

Mashing up massive government data on countless issues and the creativity of citizens will doubtlessly lead to a growing range of new services that will simplify and enrich our lives at little or no cost to government.

US OPEN GOVERNMENT INITIATIVE

When candidate Barack Obama visited Google in 2007, he pledged that, if elected, his administration would make a major commitment to transparency and open access to data. Not just data but usable data: "[We will] put government data online in universally accessible formats." [200] On his first full day in office he issued an Executive Order on Transparency and Open Government, ordering agencies to "take appropriate action, consistent with law and policy, to disclose information rapidly in forms that the public can readily find and use. Executive departments and agencies should harness new technologies to put information about their operations and decisions online and readily available to the public." [201] He followed that announcement with the March 5th, 2009 appointment of Vivek Kundra as the nation's first Chief Information Officer, charging him in part with making government as open as possible. [202]

On December 8, 2009, Obama put teeth in that order, directing agencies to come up with specific open government strategies. The memo from OMB Director Peter Orzag said the Administration's open government approach was based on three principles: transparency, participation, and collaboration. It went on to tell the agencies that within forty-five days they were to release at least three "high-value" databases via Data.gov, in forms that common web apps could easily retrieve, index and search. [203]

Each agency was also told to create an Open Government Webpage [204] that would be the gateway for all agency activities relating to the Open Government Directive.

Most important, the presumption going forward was that data should be public unless there was a compelling security and/or privacy reason to the contrary rather than the prior assumption throughout most of government that data, by definition, should be kept confidential.

Thus, by early 2010, the Obama Administration was firmly committed to a policy of openness, although critics were quick to point out any specific actions or policy omissions that ran counter to the Open Government Directive.[205]

US STIMULUS PROGRAM: OPEN DATA TURNING POINT?

Looking back at the past decade, it is obvious that the transparency and liberating data movement is gaining momentum worldwide, and that there have been enough successes both within government and within the activist community advocating for transparency to prove the approach's viability.

While it would be hard to quantify the degree of openness and access to data currently, even the most optimistic of observers feel that more data remains bottled up in inside government vaults than accessible to those who need and would benefit from it. As Clay Johnson observed, "We're about where the political campaigns were in 2004 before the first Dean Meetup."[206] On the one-year anniversary of the Obama Administration's Open Government Initiative, Sunlight's Ellen Miller, arguably the biggest cheerleader for the initiative, blasted the actual results vs. the rhetori"In its first year, the Open Government Directive made government transparency a priority and encouraged federal agencies to put important information online. While more government information is now available online, the Directive's limitations have also become clearer. Simply put, the president's commitment to transparency is not yet living up to its full potential. The Open Government Directive is a great starting point, but the hard work that is needed to create a truly open government is still ahead of us….

> ❝ *More concentrated work is needed to move beyond the easy wins. The administration has to give stronger direction and urge the agencies to move forward if the promise of an open government is to be realized."* [207]

In particular, Miller and others have been critical of data that is aggregated, released in .pdf form or other formats that make it difficult or impossible to actually work with. Their goal is to create data nuggets that exist independently of any application that may act on them.

What may really make the open data movement a priority are political realities, including the controversy over the first phase of the TARP, the $829 billion American Recovery and Reinvestment Act stimulus package, and the rise of the Tea Party movement, which demanded cuts in federal spending and more accountability for what was spent. While they come at it from opposite perspectives, activists on the left and right are watching closely how the money was spent and what the tangible results were.

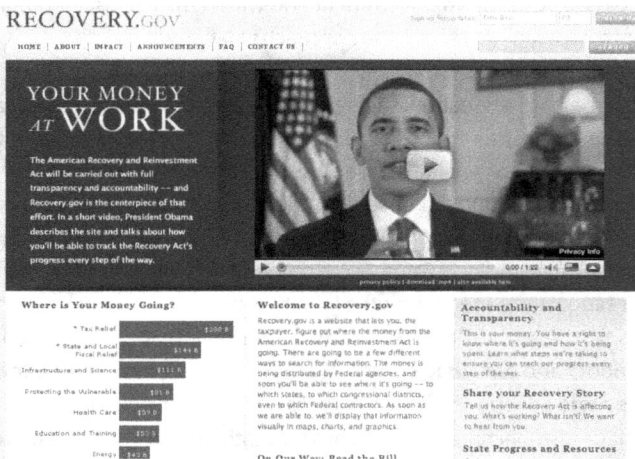

ILLUSTRATION 5-9: RECOVERY.GOV WEB SITE
Source: Recovery.gov

A month after the president signed the stimulus bill, Recovery.gov was still largely a placeholder, with general information about the law and how it would be apportioned between states and differing programs.

However, transparency activists, especially conservatives and libertarians, had already gotten a jump on Recovery.gov, with a clever crowdsourced site,Stimuluswatch,208 which was able to populate detailed pages for the shovel-ready public works projects in each state that are one of the stimulus package's

DATA DYNAMITE: How Liberating Information Will Transform Our World

centerpieces. They did this by scraping data on the projects from reports on proposed projects that mayors had filed in 2008 with the U.S. Conference of Mayors. Moreover, because the site was a wiki, users were encouraged to add additional information about the project and to vote it up or down as a priority.

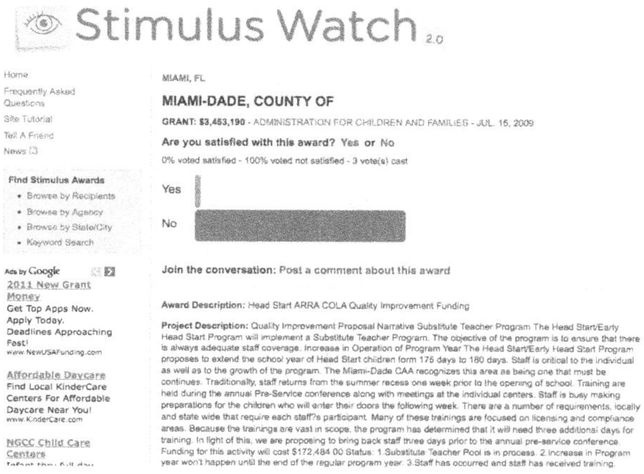

ILLUSTRATION 5-10: STIMULUSWATCH SITE
source: StimulusWatch.org

As Jerry Brito, who led the team that created StimulusWatch said, "Individuals do have the power to make change, especially when they band together in a community effort like Stimulus Watch."[209]

Brito's academic research at George Mason University's Mercatus Center also informed creation of StimulusWatch; whatever transparency and accountability steps government takes, he believes that with new Web 2.0 tools citizens must also crowdsource accountability. As he said in testimony to the House Oversight Committee regarding Recovery.gov that eloquently summarizes the logic of crowdsourcing data analysis:

> ❝ *If the government requires clear, timely, and profound reporting of how every dollar is spent, everyone—not just government auditors—could keep track of the money. Millions of citizens around the*

country would be able to look at the transactions related to recovery-funded projects in their neighborhoods. Thousands of journalists could also keep an eye on the spending and the work being done in the communities they serve. Contractors would be able to keep an eye on their competitors, and academics and watchdog groups could sift through the spending data to find interesting patterns.

❝ *Local passions, ignited by the spark of local projects, are likely to increase with the passage of time and keep all participants in the economic recovery honest and on track even after traditional watchdogs have turned their attention to the next problem.*

❝ *How would government enlist the help of citizens around the country to keep recovery spending accountable? It doesn't have to enlist help: it just has to provide data. If the government makes the raw spending data available, people across the country will build tools that allow citizens to sift, sort, and report it."*[210]

Brito is right: there's no shortage of ingenuity among the public to interpret and work with the data just as long as it's available and in usable formats.

In retrospect, the Recovery.gov website was a lost opportunity for the Obama Administration to really make transparency and open data access something that the general public could understand.[211]

For example, it was impossible for users to get an easy-to-use comprehensive view of the status of projects in their community, something that ended up hurting Democratic candidates in the 2010 election because they couldn't prove that the stimulus was actually having a demonstrable local effect. If the Obama Administration had required that the reports be in the form of structured data, and that they be available not just for governmental scrutiny but also to outside watchdog groups, the media, and average citizens, Recovery.gov could have been a major impetus for liberating data.

Even more beneficial would have been be if Recovery.gov were to be the first step in building on the FDIC and SEC requirements for reporting in XBRL. You will re-member that the architect of the Dutch Taxonomy Project was critical of the SEC mandate because it was not integrated with similar requirements for reporting to other agencies. As a result it may be seen as many companies as adding to their already onerous reporting requirements, rather than being the first step toward a fully-integrated reporting system that would actually streamline reporting. [212]

DATA.GOV: INCREASING THE FLOW OF STRUCTURED DATA FEEDS

In a teleconference the day his appointment as the nation's first CIO was an-nounced, Vivek Kundra couldn't have been more emphatic and straightforward that he would build on his D.C. Citywide Data Warehouse experience, dramatically increasing the number and variety of structured data feeds available through the new Data.gov website. He also said that the Obama Administration's default policy toward data would be to share it with the public whenever there is no compelling privacy or security reason to withhold access:

> ❝ The way I like to think about this is that if you think of two forms of data that have been published in the federal government that have fundamentally transformed the economy. One example is the National Institute of Health working with other world bodies when they published the Human Genome Project data online. What that did is it created an entire revolution in personalized medicine where you ended up having over five hundred drugs that were created and that are in the pipeline coming into the FDA.

> ❝ Second, is what happened in the geospatial community when the defense department decided to release data around satellites you created this GPS revolution where now you could go to your local car rental company and get a GPS device or your iPhone and get direc-tions.

❝ *In the same way, in the same spirit, there is a lot of data that the federal government has and what we need to do is, we need to make sure that all that data that is not private that is not restricted for national security reasons can be made public. And the question we should be thinking about even when it comes to FOIA is how do we begin with the default assumption that we put information out in the public domain then the second question is what needs to be private rather than the other way around.*"[213]

ILLUSTRATION 5-11: DATA.GOV HOMEPAGE
source: data.gov

Princeton University researcher David Robinson says that if Kundra did nothing else, simply increasing the number and diversity of public data streams would result in revolutionary change, consistent with Jerry Brito's arguments. He takes the radical position that government should de-emphasize trying to create websites that fit every user's needs, and instead concentrate on the release of structured data, which he believe the private sector and others will then craft into compelling services that focus on various groups' needs.[214]

VIRTUOUS IMITATION

Data.gov is an example of perhaps the most important aspect of most governmental open data initiatives: that they are specifically designed to be easily copied by other governmental agencies, including ones on the other side of the world.

Numerous cities in the US and elsewhere, including San Francisco, Vancouver, and Toronto, have followed the D.C. Citywide Data Warehouse model, releasing a wide range of real-time data. According to Data.gov, as of this writing, twenty-three states in the US have data sites and three other national governments, including the United Kingdom, have followed the data.gov model and released open databases.[215]

Then either through formal competitions emulating the D.C. Apps for Democracy one or just on their own, individuals and groups have created a wide variety of helpful apps capitalizing on that information.

For example, independent programmers are creating a wide range of applications as more transit authorities have emulated Washington, D.C.'s lead in releasing not just their scheduled stops but the actual real-time data that they compile from onboard transmitters that locate the current positions of buses and subways.

Each one of these new applications then becomes part of the shared knowledge base that individuals in cities that begin later to offer their real-time data can draw up. And so the cycle of virtuous imitation both continues and becomes more complex and detailed to everyone's mutual advantage.

STILL TO COME: EMPOWER WORKERS WITH REAL-TIME DATA

Where government has still not realized the full potential of sharing real-time data is in its *internal* operations, emulating Kundra's D.C. OCTO project to treat every employee as a "knowledge worker".

There was one project during the Bush Administration in the US that gave tantalizing hints of the transformational potential of such an open data strategy.

In 2007, former EPA CIO Molly O'Neill wanted a tangible project to demonstrate to EPA staffers the value of Web 2.0 social media tools. Fortunately, former EPA Administrator William Ruckelshaus, by then the Puget Sound Partnership Leadership Council's chair, also had a need: to identify and share the best ideas and tools to protect the Sound. O'Neill and Ruckelshaus collaborated, setting up an exercise for those attending the annual National Environmental Information Symposium to provide the information – in just thirty-six hours!

ILLUSTRATION 5-12: PUGET SOUND INFORMATION CHALLENGE WIKI
source: US E.P.A.

O'Neill set up a wiki to be the project's framework, and sprung the challenge on the attendees the first day. Participation was optional, but people willingly contributed, and even involved many of the people in their social networks who weren't attending.

O'Neill had already planned a mashup camp to show people how to do mashups on various EPA datasets, so she made the camp the staging area for the wiki.

While O'Neill was a little worried that no one would participate, since the project wasn't announced in advance, not only did many people at the event participate, but also they involved members of their online social networks. The event got more than 17,000 page views and more than 175 good contributions.[216]

As you can imagine, O'Neill came away convinced that this kind of voluntary project was a much more effective way of introducing Web 2.0 tools than a compulsory program would have been!

STREAMLINE BUSINESS REPORTING

Another likely trend in governmental open-data initiatives worldwide in the near future would be to streamline business reporting worldwide by following the lead of the Netherlands and Australia with unified data file reporting, to both cut companies' compliance costs and to allow coordinated interagency review. The Obama Administration has pledged rigorous regulatory enforcement in reaction to lax regulatory oversight in the Bush Administration, but that doesn't have to mean that it be accomplished through burdensome twentieth-century style reports.

As a result of the 2010 U.S. elections, Rep. Darrell Issa (R-CA) chairs the House Subcommittee on Oversight and Reform, and that is likely to spur adoption of more use of XBRL in the U.S., and SBR in particular. Issa not only advocates use of XBRL, but he really understands the standard and its potential. He filed a bill that would have required tagging all reports to the government from banks receiving Toxic Asset Relief Program (TARP) funds with XBRL to let government officials and the public track the use of TARP funds and unlock the value of toxic mortgage assets.[217] Another bill that Issa filed would require all government agencies to adopt a uniform financial data standard for both their internal financial information and whatever financial information they collected from the private sector in regulatory filings.

Even before assuming his new post, Issa warned that it was time to switch to XBRL-based reporting. In a *Washington Enquirer* op-ed, he wrote that federal agencies don't use consistent standards now in reporting their financial activities, and, if they did, "and made it all public, searchable, sortable, and downloadable, anyone with web access could scrutinize the federal budget, second-guess federal regulators, or navigate proposed laws and the U.S. Code with ease."

He went on to say:

" Consistent data formats and reliable public access would give the public a better understanding of their government's actions. Such knowledge is essential for the federal government to earn the informed consent of the governed, which is a basic principle of democracy. Indeed, transparency through technology presents a real opportunity to begin controlling spending, simplifying the bureaucracy, and regaining the confidence of the American people." [218]

I've written elsewhere that an XBRL-based regulation system — what I called Regulation 3.0 — might be an ideal 21st-century replacement to the lax, hard-to-enforce regulatory systems that have been shown inadequate in situations such as the 2010 BP oil spill. The key would be the "Internet of Things" that I explain in Chapter 6, in which components of an oil rig or other regulated process would have built-in low-power transmitters and each component would have its own Internet Protocol (IP) address. The company would benefit because it would no longer have to compile and file written reports on its activity: that would be done automatically as the equipment operates. The company would also benefit because it would get real-time information from the equipment that would allow it to adjust flows, predict needed maintenance, and coordinate with its supply chain. Meanwhile, the government would no longer have to wait until the company reports to get information on its performance: the agency would get the same data the company is getting, and on a real-time basis. If, as in the case of BP, it ignored warnings from the regulatory agency that its operations were at risk, the agency would have the ability to pre-emptively shut the process down to avoid a disaster.

CURRENT STATE-OF-THE-ART: FEDERAL REGISTER 2.0

While the Sunlight Foundation has its gripes with data.gov, one Obama initiative it heartily endorses, and which nicely embodies the key components of open data release, is the Federal Register 2.0 portal.

If you're not familiar with the Federal Register, it's probably because it was so arcane and hard to read in its print form (which totals more than 80,000 pages a year) and even in the early web-based version. The Federal Register is the federal government's "daily paper," the place where agencies publish things such as proposed and final rules, public notices, and actions by the president. Doubtless, given the content, it would have much wider readership, especially among those tracking a specific issue or interested in responding to agencies' requests for proposals, if it were easier to navigate.

The first step in the transition was to release the Federal Register tagged with XML, beginning in October 2009, with access backdated to 2000, something open data pioneer Carl Malamud had been advocating for years. As the Open Government Initiative blog post announcing the change emphasized: "With an XML edition, independent organizations can reorganize the Register's contents in ways that are more meaningful to you and address your personal interests; track issues that are likely to affect your community or your profession; and even engage in real-time public discussions about its contents with others across the country and around the world."[219]

Capitalizing on the feed, several activists, including Malamud, immediately launched services such as Fedthread.org, which allows users to annotate the Federal Register and comment in its margins or software application that makes it simpler to search the Federal Register.

On July 26, 2010, the seventy-fifth anniversary of the Federal Register, the next step in the Register's online evolution was launched. Its development illustrated a key component of liberating data: the cross-fertilization and synergies that can occur among all sectors when they all have access to the same data. That's especially true for those such as the DevelopmentSEED team in Chapter 1 or other small companies or activist groups that are long on enthusiasm and ingenuity but short on financial resources. The three solo programmers who banded together to win Sunlight Labs' second Apps for America Contest, with another version of the Register, GovPulse.us, were asked by the two agencies responsible for the Federal Register to help in building the new site (that kind of informal working relationship was, needless to say, a refreshing alternative to the normal government procurement process!).[220]

The new site is as user-friendly as the print Federal Register is intimidating. As the news release announcing the project said, the Register site "emerges today in a new 21st Century format thaz for the first time will allow readers to sift through, reorganize, and electronically customize its daily contents".

ILLUSTRATION 5-13: NEW FEDERAL REGISTER SITE
source: Federal Register

Continuing the "government's daily paper" theme, the home page resembles that of an online paper, with six major sections (money, environment, world, science and technology, business and industry, and health and public welfare). Individual documents (referred to as "articles") are selected by both the agencies' editorial judgment and user interest, or they may get preferred positioning because of crowdsourced interest by users. Each major federal agency has its own homepage, which describes its mission and selected information, such as "Significant Rules," and a collection of both its most recent and most cited articles.

Because encouraging public comment on various proposed regulations is supposed to be a major reason for the Register, there's a calendar tool that gives comment period opening and ending dates, public meeting dates and other public participation options. In the past, some major contractors have had employees whose major responsibility was combing the Federal Register for contracting opportunities, so this new easy-to-search format levels the playing field for smaller companies.

The ability to search the Register was a major focus. There's a search box at the top

DATA DYNAMITE: How Liberating Information Will Transform Our World

of every page, readers can subscribe to a variety of searches for automatic delivery to their desktops, including a search term, a section or an agency. One can even for any articles that affect a geographic region within X miles of a given ZIP Code.

It also uses graphs, charts and maps and other visual data representations.

Perhaps most important in terms of maximizing the site's usability, it was created entirely using open source tools and the code was made available for anyone to improve on. Each Federal Register document also includes a link to the corresponding raw XML file for free use in other applications.

SERIOUS THREAT, OR SHORT-TERM OBSTACLE?

Just as *Data Dynamite* was going to press, we learned that the historic $38 billion U.S. budget cut included reducing funding for open data programs such as Data. gov, from $34 million in FY 2010 to $2 million in FY 2011. The Sunlight Foundation and others worry that the even more draconian FY 2012 budget may cut them even further. The only glimmer of hope is that Rep. Issa has given a personal pledge that he will try to use his power as chairman of the Committee on Oversight and Government Reform to save the programs.

As dire as these cuts are for the immediate future of transparency programs on the federal level in the U.S., I remain optimistic about the future worldwide, because the barriers to entry for new programs are increasingly low because of the ability to copy the early adopters. I may be naïve, but I can't help thinking that liberals and conservatives, even though they may support transparency for different reasons, can find common ground and preserve at least basic programs of this sort.

IBM'S "SMARTER PLANET": DATA-DRIVEN SYSTEMS THINKING

One government contractor that definitely grasps data's central role in delivering more efficient, less costly services is IBM. According to IBM Chairman and CEO Sam Palmisano, data is being captured today as never before:

❝ *Data…reveals everything from large and systemic patterns—of global markets, workflows, national infrastructures and natural systems—to the location, temperature, security and condition of every item in a global supply chain. And then there's the growing torrent of information from billions of individuals using social media. They are customers, citizens, students and patients. They are telling us what they think, what they like and want, and what they're witnessing. As important, all this data is far more real-time than ever before.*

❝ *And here's the key point: data by itself isn't useful. Over the past year we have validated what we believed would be true—and that is, the most important aspect of smarter systems is data—and, more specifically, the actionable insights that the data can reveal. We have seen the emergence of a kind of global data field. The planet itself has always generated an enormous amount of data, but we didn't used to be able to hear it, to see it, to capture it. Now we can because all of this stuff is now instrumented. And it's all interconnected, so now we can actually have access to it. So, in effect, the planet has grown a central nervous system."*[221]

I have not read a more powerful endorsement of the central role of real-time data in smart management of complex systems.

IBM's "Smarter Planet" initiative is bringing about major efficiency and cost-saving benefits for client cities around the world by giving city workers access to real-time data that helps reduce inefficiency, improve interagency collaboration, and see patterns in operational problems that were invisible without the perspective data analysis can bring.

The program grew out of one of IBM's "Jam Factory" programs, a company-wide online innovation brainstorming session. The company decided to fund "Big Green Tech," which would apply IBM technology to reducing carbon emissions and saving water.

Separately, IBM management looked at whether the company had relevant expertise that could make green initiatives a new line of business.

Dr. Colin Harrison, director of IBM Enterprise Initiatives, headed a team that determined there were "clear patterns to issues such as water, energy and transportation", and advised that IBM's competitive advantage could come from guess what? Data!

He suggested that they build a middleware platform, capture data from sensors monitoring the various issues, and then do analytics to try to detect usage patterns, opportunities for saving, and so on. Known as the "Instrumented Planet Study", this program became part of what was eventually labeled the Smarter Planet initiative. [222]

The first specific project that Smarter Planet was called in on was Masdar City, the planned environmentally-sound community in the United Arab Emirates. It was planned from the beginning to run entirely on energy from photovoltaics and other renewable sources.[223] "We concluded that a single unified data platform in the same place could unify management of the transportation, energy, water, and public safety programs", Harrison says. He elaborated, "We rarely deal directly with the sensors monitoring various operating conditions: it's the data coming from those sensors that speaks to us."[224]

The major lesson that emerges from the Smarter Planet's experiences to date is the importance of systems thinking, in which the old linear thinking and dealing with various issues in isolation is replaced by an approach in which the relationship between various issues, such as energy and the environment, is most important, and solutions aim at holistic approaches addressing all of the factors simultaneously.

One project that demonstrates the benefits of the data-centric, systems-thinking approach is IBM's work for one of its smaller clients, the city of Corpus Christi, Texas.

It would have been hard for any city to have been more behind the times in handling citizen complaints than Corpus Christi was: each department used to have its own complaint system, and they recorded calls on 3 x 5 cards.

Now the city has an intelligent citywide system unifying all of the departments' responses: administrators see all hotspots on a digital map, and plan responses on a real-time basis.

Perhaps the most dramatic example of how data analytics can reveal previously invisible patterns was that they found one-third of the water department's responses concerned only one percent of the system. They focused on that area for improvements, dramatically reducing the number of complaints.

As the Smarter Planet CTO, Guru Banavar, wrote about the program, "I think Steve Klepper of Corpus Christi captures this concept best when he talks about a city as a collection of data points streets, bridges, parks, buildings, fire hydrants, water mains, and storm water ditches. If you manage your data, you can measure it, and improve it continuously". [225]

While Smarter Planet is an IBM profit center, the company insists that one key to improving cities' operations is coming up with open standards for data sharing, so it is likely other cities that aren't IBM clients can benefit from the innovations just as they do with other open standards-based projects. [226]

DOING MORE WITH LESS: DUSTIN HAISLER

As with other chapters in Data Dynamite, this one will conclude with an example of liberating data under extreme conditions. In this case the extreme condition was lack of funding, which required ingenuity to cope with.

Meet Dustin Haisler, until recently the IT director for the city of Manor, Texas, an

Austin suburb with a population of six thousand.[227]

What Haisler managed to do on a budget of less than $100,000 is astonishing and has drawn worldwide attention.

Haisler's particular claim to fame is his creative use of Quick Response (QR) codes, the two-dimensional variation on barcodes that began in Japan and is quickly becoming adopted here due in no small part to the publicity Haisler's work has received. [228]

He and the mayor were looking for a cheap way to record the location and contents of paper records stored in boxes. They hit upon QR codes, which, unlike conventional bar codes, have the advantage of being free: you can just print them yourself.

Once Haisler and the mayor had labeled the records boxes, they were intrigued: couldn't QR codes be used elsewhere, and couldn't the ability to store up to seven thousand characters be used other ways? Soon the codes were appearing everywhere in Manor, from police cars to public works projects, where all sorts of details on project funding, names and phone numbers of contractors, and so on, could be found.

Haisler says a major goal was transparency:

> ❝ By placing QR-code signs at each of our construction projects, we can provide the taxpayer real-time information about that project.... When there were costs or timeframe changes...we would only have to update the information on the website because the QR-code hyper-link remained the same.

> ❝ Instead of bombarding our residents with information they don't want through traditional means of communication, we have created

a model of information dissemination that puts them in the driver's

seat and engages them to get involved."[229]

"Engages" is the key word: when Haisler and the city manager had the brainstorming session that led to the QR initiative, the goal they articulated as the means to economic growth for the city was an unorthodox one: "Make Manor more engaging". Thus, everything they have done has been aimed at breaking down barriers between government and the people, whether through interactive tours of downtown or creation of Manor Labs to crowdsource ideas.

As part of its effort to become truly data-centric, Manor plans to eventually tie the QR system to its work orders.

The city has its own innovation lab, Manor Labs, and tries to develop cheap, open source solutions to its needs rather than buying expensive, proprietary programs.

Citizens have responded very positively: Manor Labs is built on crowdsourcing, constantly soliciting residents' (although anyone anywhere can also contribute) ideas on new information services. The ideas go through a four-step winnowing process, and the best ones receive "Inno Bucks", an ersatz money form that entitles them to a variety of small rewards, even including a dinner from a local restaurant or to be "mayor for a day". One of the most popular ideas was a downtown beautification project that included most traditional aspects of such programs, but added a distinctly Manor touch: a driving tour featuring "narration" from the QR code signs. Another suggestion was to launch a community-based effort to document to chains that the city could support a supermarket, and that in turn led to a discussion of what kinds of social practices a chain should have if Manor were to solicit its business.

If six-thousand-person Manor, Texas can develop all these great ideas on a budget under $100,000, what excuses do other government agencies have for not following suit?

CHAPTER 6

DATA-CENTRIC COMPANIES

When you think about it, the accomplishments of many companies in the past were nothing short of miraculous.

After all, the problems with gathering and disseminating data we've discussed earlier meant that their management and employees had to make decisions every day about all sorts of critical issues based only on fragmentary information. Most of what information they did have was only historical. As a result, data inevitably was thought of only as an adjunct to decision-making rather than as a critical factor to always consider.

Even in those cases where real-time information was available, the cost of gathering, distributing, and processing it was so high that only wealthy companies could afford the cost of giving senior management access to that information and the tools such as business intelligence (BI) dashboards to interpret and act on it.

That, of course, was despite the fact that it is usually the rank-and-file staff who as part of performing their daily responsibilities must make decisions that have immediate effects on operations, and who would benefit most from access to real-time data. They didn't get what they needed.

When it came to designing products and services, those companies were also operating in the dark. They could use focus groups and other tools to gauge customer opinion. However, they were invariably limited to designing products and services that were compromises, meant to generally satisfy most consumers rather than truly meeting the specific needs of individual customers and delighting them in the process.

Even though those limitations on access to real-time data and tools to work with it have been eliminated, only a handful of companies have had the vision to capitalize on liberating data's potential to improve decision making, reduce costs by unprecedented coordination with supply chains, and create new mass-customized products. Perhaps it is because these companies have become so conditioned to limited data that their horizons have been permanently constrained. Or, they are still stuck in the old business paradigm that says data must be hoarded and kept secret, even though there's increasing evidence that under the new rules, data becomes more valuable when it is shared, and loses value when it isn't!

To try to overcome that limited vision, we will examine the various components of an integrated, data-centric enterprise. Examining the benefits a few companies have achieved by undertaking initiatives in one or more aspects of it will underscore the potential (while realizing that achieving the full benefits of a data-centric strategy can only be achieved by a comprehensive, holistic approach embracing all of these characteristics). Looking at several new companies that have been created specifically to exploit real-time data will vividly demonstrate the entrepreneurial opportunities for those who grasp this transformation.

Finally, we will see that one of the best current examples of such a data-centric company is in an industry more noted for its ignorance of modern communications in a country rarely known for management innovation. If a Mexican concrete company can do it, why can't yours?

THE KEY TO FINALLY ACHIEVING LONG-SOUGHT RE-FORMS

For years, management theorists and innovative companies have pursued four elusive goals that we've come to realize are interrelated:

1. Squeeze inefficiency out of internal and supply chain processes by closer integration and information sharing.

2. Improve corporate operations by giving all employees (not just élites) the real-time information they need to make better decisions.

3. Create feedback loops that will help companies better respond to customers, fine-tune their products and services, and react to changing conditions.

4. Improve quality by more precise monitoring of production.

A brief review of some of the leading theorists' work will remind us of the priorities they have established.

DEMING

W. Edwards Deming pioneered the concept of statistical process control to improve quality, and emphasized feedback loops for continuous improvement (what he called "plan-do-check-act"). Japanese industries embraced the approach long before US firms did.[230]

SIX SIGMA PROGRAMS

Begun by Motorola, they build on Deming's work through an emphasis on removing defects and tightly controlling and systematizing production processes. Six Sigma also emphasizes rigorous statistical analysis, and relies on specially trained analysts to interpret data, with a goal of 99.99966% defect-free products.[231]

MAJOR JOHN BOYD'S OODA LOOP

A matter of life or death, Boyd created the OODA loop (Observe, Orient, Decide and Act) to help improve fighter pilots' effectiveness and survival rate. It is a continuous, cyclical process. The pilot observes conditions, analyzes them, changes tactics depending on the enemy's tactics, acts and then repeats the process endlessly. The OODA Loop has since been applied to corporate decision-making.[232]

PETER SENGE'S LEARNING ORGANIZATION

Senge says that what he calls the "learning organization" is one in which management actively encourages the entire workforce to learn and innovate. It looks at management and production issues in terms of "systems dynamics," in which everything is linked by feedback loops to foster continuous improvement. [233]

GARTNER'S ZERO-LATENCY ENTERPRISE (ZLE)

It aims for instantaneous awareness and appropriate responses to events across an entire enterprise. New information entered into any application is instantly available to all who might need it. A major challenge to implementing all of these theories was that access to the data needed to make these changes was always limited (like the situation with written manuscripts in the days prior to Luther). In part this was because of cost and the sheer difficulty of gathering and disseminating the data, but also because most workers, lacking a background in statistics, wouldn't be able to interpret the data even if they had access to it. Even where there were significant advances, they relied on costly, proprietary systems that were limited in their use to only the most affluent companies.

However, just as Luther freed the Bible from the monks and gave people tools to communicate, the barriers to real-time access to data and interpretive tools have been removed.

An explosion similar to what Luther unleashed with the printed word is now likely for empowered workers' use of data.

For the first time, it is now possible for *all* workers to have access, when and where they need it, to information that will help them do their jobs better. As David Siegel wrote in *Pull* describing the shift to data-on-demand, "We automatically get what we need when we need it".[235]

Product and service design can benefit from closed-loop systems in which customers' feedback provides valuable insights into their interests and behavior, allowing further improvements or even mass-customization of products for every individual. At the same time, automated delivery of real-time information can help integrate supply chains, make split-second changes in the flow of pipelines, and even allow real-time pricing changes in reaction to market changes.

TWO SHIFTS TO REALIZE FULL BENEFITS OF LIBERATING DATA

As important to reforming business as access to real-time data and tools to use will be, your company will never realize the full benefits of liberating data unless it you make two critical attitudinal shifts.

[1] PROVIDE UNIVERSAL DATA ACCESS TO ALL WHO NEED IT

Universal access means *universal* access.

Even start-up companies (in fact, perhaps especially start-ups, which aren't encumbered by legacy systems and can structure their systems and procedures from day one to assure everyone gets access to the data they need) need to provide data access to their entire workforce.

Companies must begin from the assumption that data should be shared with all those who would be able to do their jobs within the company more effectively if they had that access.

It also must also be shared with companies, even small ones, who are their suppliers and customers. Walmart's Retail Link inventory system lets its suppliers see exactly how many of their products are on every store's shelves *in real time*. In some cases the supplier actually manages the restocking, and Walmart avoids tying up money in inventory. As Fingar and Bellini wrote in *Real-Time Enterprise* describing Walmart's commitment to data sharing with its entire supply chain: "By beaming demand signals in real time to all its suppliers, Walmart enables the entire value chain to respond to actual demand, rather than to forecast. Forecasts, by definition, are wrong. It's this information chain on steroids that allows products to flow from manufacturers to consumer without being unduly imprisoned in Walmart warehouses". [236]

[2] CREATE A CULTURE OF COLLABORATION AND EMPOWERMENT

Equally important, achieving the full benefit of the data-centric enterprise can't be achieved without a spirit of collaboration and both organizational structures and tools to encourage it. As we will see later in this chapter with the innovative $1 million Netflix Prize, it was adding former competitors to the teams that resulted in the top entries.

That means, most of all, that all we've assumed in the past about the value of proprietary information and the role of managers as information gatekeepers, must be re-thought.

In the new era, managers will intervene to control data only when it is vital. And, once given access to the data, workers must be given decision-making authority to act on it. So managers' role must evolve to being facilitators of collaboration and empowerment.

SIX CHARACTERISTICS OF COMPANIES THAT LIBERATE DATA

Companies that effectively liberate data in this new era will have six primary characteristics. A look at companies that are pioneering new policies and procedures to bring about some form of universal data access will illustrate the benefits of the transition.

[1] DATA IS AUTOMATICALLY TAGGED WITH METADATA THE VERY FIRST TIME IT IS ENTERED ANYWHERE IN THE COMPANY AND THEN AUTOMATICALLY DISTRIBUTED.

That will remove the need to frequently re-enter the same data in multiple programs and places throughout the company, not only reducing errors and labor, but also assuring that as soon as the data is changed, it will be instantly updated everywhere it is needed.

Remember, the Holy Grail is that data is only entered once! Just think what an effect that would have every aspect of your operations.

Later in this chapter you will learn about Vitality, Inc., a start-up that is dramatically increasing patients' compliance taking prescribed drugs by means of its "GlowCap" for prescription containers.

Vitality Vice-President for Software Development Jamie Biggar says the company tags data sent from the caps as soon as it enters their servers. It is stored in a way so that the original data is always preserved, no matter how it is also digested and analyzed. "The data is never re-entered. The raw data flows into the database along with its metadata and is never modified so retains its integrity no matter what. Maintaining raw canonical data integrity is crucial!" according to Biggar. [237]

Of course it is easier for a start-up such as Vitality to tag its data instantly, but software tools are available to make it possible for established companies, with legacy systems, to do the same.

[2] THE COMPANY IS "DATA-CENTRIC".

That's both literally and figuratively true: these companies will routinely map their internal processes in ways showing data at the heart of everything the company does, with all its processes and employees accessing data directly, rather than indirectly and filtered by processes and managers.[238] Visualizing data's centrality will constantly remind staff to honor that practice in everything they do.

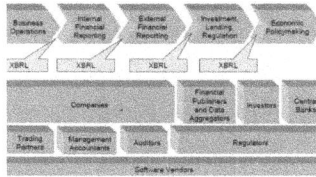

ILLUSTRATION 6-1: DATA-CENTRIC ORGANIZATION
source: Hitachi

Equally important, the company will promote a culture of data awareness, in which all employees have a rudimentary understanding of data and how to interpret it. Every company will be more like Walmart, where CIO Rollin Ford says, "Every day I wake up and ask, 'How can I flow data better, manage data better, analyze data better?'"[239]

They will also have both Web 2.0 collaboration tools and data visualization tools that will encourage collaborative analysis of data. Because more perspectives will be represented in the decision-making process, decisions will be more fully formed and nuanced. Because of the ease of sharing data, everyone will routinely ask themselves and others: where else could this data create value? Inevitably, the uses (and their value) will multiply.

I can't emphasize enough how profound that shift would be: the simple act of asking where else the data could be used and making it available there will inevitably turn our strategic vision outward, rather than inward, and promote collaboration and mutual gain.

The Container Store empowers every employee at the individual store level by providing them with the latest sales data at twice-daily "huddles" where everyone, not just managers, reviews the prior day's sales at that store as well as chain-wide, and discusses sales targets for the day. At the after-closing huddle, the manager tells whether or not the store met the target, breaking the total down by individual departments, and encourages discussion among employees regarding their individual observations on what happened that day and how lessons learned could be applied to improve sales.

[3] THE ORGANIZATION GAINS A COMPETITIVE ADVANTAGE FROM REAL-TIME OPERATIONS.

It will streamline its operations and integrate more closely with its customers and suppliers. Because the customers and suppliers will also use the same global standards for structuring data, it will be easily shared. The advantages will range from reducing inventory and cost-per-transaction, to real-time re-engineering of processes.[240]

Perhaps the best example today of real-time data sharing's benefits is the symbiotic relationship between Walmart and P&G (although it is nowhere near as powerful as a free, open-standard-based system such as XBRL) because their system relies on an expensive proprietary electronic data interchange (EDI) system that is beyond the budget of most companies.

The two companies created a continuous replenishment process (CRP) that P&G, not Walmart, actually controls.

Both companies benefit. Walmart reduces inventory because P&G now manages the frequency and size of deliveries, rather than waiting for Walmart to make an order. P&G increased its sales to Walmart by 32.5% because its analysis of Walmart point-of-sale data revealed there were fifty-six items Walmart carried that didn't sell well; P&G also suggested that Walmart carry twenty-five products that did sell well.[241]

The system illustrates a key point about the data-centric organization: instead of jealously guarding information, it can be more profitable to share it with suppliers. This allows much closer integration of activities and allows a cyclical process rather than the old linear order-and-delivery one. In the case of Walmart and P&G, contrast inventory before and after the new system was implemented:

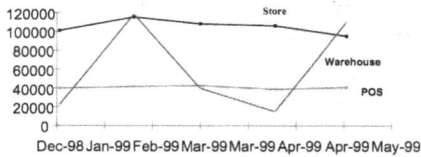

ILLUSTRATION 6-2 INVENTORY LEVELS BEFORE AND AFTER DATA SHARING
source: E-business management

The systems are so well integrated that most items P&G ships are in a Walmart warehouse for less than eight hours, on a Walmart shelf within four hours, and sold within a day! That lets Walmart collect revenues from consumers buying the products before Walmart has to pay the suppliers, or what retailers call "negative cash-to-cash cycle times".[242]

[4] MANUFACTURING AND PROCESS EQUIPMENT SHARE DATA INSTANTLY, OFTEN WITHOUT HUMAN INTERVENTION, USING WEB 3.0 "INTERNET OF THINGS" TECHNOLOGY.

With the "Internet of Things", refrigerators, assembly-line equipment, and all matter of other devices will have their own Internet Protocol (IP)[243] address, sensors to detect current operating conditions, and built-in low-power transmitters so that operational data will be broadcast continuously. This real-time data will allow the company to operate at peak efficiency and spot maintenance issues before they can become serious.

This is not a pipe dream. FedEx is already gaining a strategic advantage in the fiercely competitive delivery business by using "Internet of Things" devices. In 2010 it launched the SenseAwareTM tag[244] to provide real-time tracking of a wide range of highly valuable items en route, from time-critical items such as organs for transplants to highly-regulated ones such as materials requiring chain-of-custody certification.

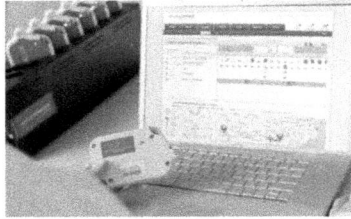

The tag uses proven technology (an accelerometer to detect movement, GPS to establish location, cellular transmitter), in a novel combination, adding a thermometer and light sensor, so that it can relay in real time exactly what is happening to these types of precious cargoes and their exact location in the air or on the ground.

Because FedEx operates its own fleet of planes and thus controls all the data transmission factors, it could convince the FAA that the data transmission from the devices would not affect navigation information, so it received a waiver allowing the sensors to operate while in flight.[245]

Given how sensitive these kinds of items can be to any variations in conditions during shipment, if FedEx can document that they were handled within acceptable parameters, that information would be of tremendous value to shippers (and, of course, could let FedEx charge a premium: the first-generation devices cost $120 monthly).

Equally important, because the Web transmits it, the data is shared instantly between all involved: shipper, FedEx, and recipient. A browser-based collaboration tool allows all parties to work together immediately if they must react to changing conditions such as an increase in temperature.

As described by FedEx, the potential applications in the early stages of implementing the system are ones where real-time data is critical (or even a matter of life or death). For example, they would include situations where an implant had to be maintained at a certain temperature while on its way to an operation, pharmaceutical companies that have to assure secure and temperature-sensitive distribution from the plant to doctors' offices, or all participants in a clinical trial where both protection of the samples and precise record-keeping was critical. [246]

It can easily provide users with real-time data such as whether the package has gotten too hot or cold, or whether light struck the interior of the package (indicating it had been opened). As *ReadWriteWeb* observed, "Essentially, the SenseAware events will trigger business processes for users," demonstrating exactly how powerful these devices are. That power is derived specifically because of their ability to generate and report real-time, actionable data. [247]

[5] LINEAR PROCESSES BECOME CYCLICAL.

In the data-centric company, feedback data is quickly factored into changes in product design and delivery. In many cases, customers can take a direct role in product design.

Blank Label, a custom shirt start-up, capitalizes on automatic data flow to keep its costs to a minimum while simultaneously delighting customers.

ILLUSTRATION 6-4: BLANK LABEL SHIRT DESIGNED BY THE AUTHOR
source: Blanklabel

For anyone still operating under the illusion that data just equals cold, hard facts, consider that Blank Label founder Fan Bi says the key to the company's approach is that "People really like a Blank Label shirt because they can say, 'I had a part in creating this,' by choosing among a whole range of options including fabric, collar style, and even whether to omit a pocket".[248]

[6] COMPANIES SHARE SOME OF THEIR MOST IMPORTANT DATA WITH OTHER COMPANIES AND EVEN WITH THE PUBLIC.

Data-centric companies realize that when selected data is shared, it often leads to greater profits than if it is kept proprietary.

In 1789 young Sam Slater left England and came to the US with something important on his mind. He'd skillfully gotten around a British law making it illegal to take plans for the early woolen mills abroad by *memorizing* those plans. When he got to the US, Slater built factories throughout New England and became the father of the US textile industry.

In the past, keeping your company's information secret (as the British textile industry tried to do) was the way to profitability: you could make money by exploiting it and doling out little "nuggets" of information at opportune times. The last thing you would think of would be (gasp!) giving it away.

Open-source software led the way toward the data-sharing paradigm shift. Users were dissatisfied with proprietary software, particularly the way that the companies' marketing needs, rather than users' needs, dictated the timing of the release of major upgrades. Instead, with open source, versioning became continuous, because a group created and released it. Perhaps originally dubious, users began to see how much more robust the open-source programs could be.

Now, access to data is also undergoing a paradigm shift from jealously guarding it to sharing it.

Don Tapscott and Anthony Williams' *Wikinomics* is full of examples of companies that have experimented with what they call "mass collaboration", particularly involving companies such as P& G that have taken some of their most prized corporate assets—proprietary data—and divulged it externally to solicit alternative ideas about how to profitably capitalize on that data. [249]

Perhaps nothing demonstrates that paradigm shift better than the Netflix Prize, a perfect demonstration of the two fundamental marks of a data-centric organization: make data widely available unless there is a compelling reason not to, and then analyze and act on that data collaboratively.

Netflix became the leader in online video rentals in large part because of its proprietary Cinematch algorithm, which lets it make helpful suggestions to customers about what other movies they might enjoy, based on their past rentals and those of others with similar profiles.

So you can imagine management must have taken a deep breath in 2006 when they released 100,480,507 past ratings by users (yes, that data was tagged!) as the working material for the Netflix Prize, a winner-take-all, open-ended contest that would award $1 million to the team that was the first to come up with a new algorithm that would be at least ten per cent more accurate than Cinematch.[250] The contest concluded in September 2009. "BellKor's Pragmatic Chaos", which combined two teams, "Bellkor in BigChaos", and "Pragmatic Theory", won the final prize.

Greg McAlpin, a member of the second-place team, The Ensemble, said Netflix took a crucial step when launching the contest: creating forums where people could ask questions of Netflix and share ideas.[251] That set a tone of openness and collaboration that shaped much of what was to happen during the contest. From start to finish, the entire competition was marked by innovative strategies and team-building approaches that would be totally inexplicable to companies used to competition at all costs, but which I predict will become commonplace in the era of the data-centric organization.

As the contest heated up in early 2009, McAlpin put up a Drupal site, the Probe File Exchange, and invited six competitors to join. "They were not chosen because they had the lowest scores. They were chosen because they were all active on the Netflix forum and their posts were consistently helpful, friendly, and funny. They were chosen because they are the sort of people that you want to work with."[252] Other collaborative efforts accelerated, leading to mergers of several teams.

On June 26, 2009 "BellKor's Pragmatic Chaos" achieved the goal: a 10.05% improvement over Cinematch. Under the competition's complicated rules, that triggered a thirty-day period in which all the teams could make a final submission.

ILLUSTRATION 6-5: FINAL LEADERBOARD FOR NETFLIX PRIZE
source: Netflix

McAlpin's retelling of what The Ensemble did during that period has a surreal tone in light of how slowly and deliberately corporate alliances and mergers are usually negotiated in the old economy. He casually tosses off an incredible array of steps they took throughout the month, as if the clock wasn't ticking (and rather loudly!). They continued the pattern they'd established before, contacting everyone they'd talked to earlier, adding two key team members and even inviting the leaders, "BellKor's Pragmatic Chaos", to join (why not, I guess!).

Astonishingly, because the whole competition was data driven, making those changes on the fly was critical. The incremental improvements the new members contributed meant that with *four minutes* left in the competition, the Ensemble submitted an entry that beat BellKor by .01%.

It wasn't over yet. Under the rules, a second round of secret tests by Netflix resulted in a slightly higher score for BellKor, giving them the prize.[253]

It's too complex to recount here, but I strongly urge you to listen to McAlpin's reading at the South by Southwest conference from his diary of the last six months of the competition.[254] Granted, putting together *ad hoc* teams for the sole purpose of competing for a prize differs tremendously from managing a company for years of sustained performance, but I think it gives a preview of how working and manag-

DATA DYNAMITE: How Liberating Information Will Transform Our World

ing in the era of liberated data will differ radically from the past:

→ Alliances will be made and broken on a real-time basis, without lawyers' intervention.

→ Competitors will also be collaborators.

→ Real-time shared access to data will allow instant changes to work products, without the old reviews up the chain of command.

As Chris Hefele, another member of The Ensemble team commented, they were aware that the challenges were as much organizational as technical, and that their willingness to embrace innovative collaboration methods was crucial. "It's my opinion that the successes of this team is not only being driven by the technologies we're using to combine or data, but also by our ability to combine many people together and create a cohesive, functioning team in less than thirty days. So our successes will be not only technological, but also organizational. It will be interesting to see if a large group of underdogs can defeat a small group of the leaders." [255]

JUMP-STARTING THE PROCESS

In his great preview of the semantic web transition, *Pull*, David Siegel previews the astounding changes possible simply by tagging data. He recounts how dramatically the process that banks use to report to the Federal Deposit Insurance Corporation evolved after they were required to add XBRL tags to the data.

When the XBRL tagging requirement began in 2005, the FDIC sent the banks the entire taxonomy, including the terms, definitions and business rules required for compliance. Because these rules were formulated using the XBRL tags, the banks could "catch all the logic and math errors, so banks couldn't send in a faulty report".[256]

The change was easily implemented. It cost only $40 million, all 8,200 banks that were required to file the reports adopted the new approach, and there was both a one-hundred-percent compliance rate and one-hundred-percent reduction in logic and math errors.

For the average bank, instead of the forty-five days after the close of a quarter it took to report previously, the reports were now filed in less than fifteen days. Some banks even file their call reports within a day! Siegel predicts that, "Eventually, the FDIC could eliminate the requirement for quarterly reports entirely, going to continuous reporting that is simply a byproduct of doing business".[257]

Astoundingly to me, given the ease of implementing XBRL-based reporting the FDIC change demonstrated, few companies use it at this point for anything more than filing reports to regulatory agencies such as the FDIC or SEC.

In the future, visionary companies will turn XBRL into a real management tool, achieving goals such as real-time cash management. The tag system to create such a robust reporting tool for internal use (XBRL Global Ledger, or XBR GL) is an extended version of the XBRL that publicly-traded companies must already use to report to the SEC and banks must use for FDIC reports. Using the extended version internally amortizes the time and effort that went into creating those XBRL-based reports.[258] As David Siegel says, if companies used XBRL internally for their daily operations, internal as well as governmental reporting would be a mere formality: "Just by doing business your books are done and your reports are filed".[259]

WHY DOES WACOAL STAND ALONE?

Wacoal, the Japanese apparel conglomerate, was the first company to implement XBRL GL to run its daily operations, not just file government reports. It was an innovation born of necessity: the company grew through acquisitions to the point that it was faced with integrating reporting from the thirty-two legacy accounting systems of thirty-six subsidiaries into a new company-wide Oracle system, and to do so on a budget.[260]

A wide range of problems plagued the old patchwork process, each of which a unified XBRL GL system addressed. Not only was there a variety of systems, but also data entry was only partially automated, so employees had to extract data from vouchers and input it manually. That increased personnel costs and increased errors, especially when the same data had to be entered into multiple systems. When there was an error, it was hard to trace. Similar activities, such as assigning customer order and return numbers, were handled differently by each division.

In short, Wacoal's situation typified the limitations of current, fragmentary data entry and use that companies of all sizes and types have come to accept as the normal way to do business.

It doesn't have to be and the solution is cost effective.

It's important for companies dealing with duplicative, incompatible systems to realize that tagging with XBRL offers a low-cost alternative to the daunting challenge of scrapping legacy systems and starting over. The Hitachi-based XBRL GL system that Wacoal implemented allowed them to keep the old systems, and simply enter their unique business rules into the add-on. Now all the data from all the system flows into the common company-wide Oracle system. It's used for a wide range of data: purchasing, sales, inventory, materials, and workflow.

Wacoal achieved important strategic goals as well, including improved support for decision-making and reducing indirect costs. At the end of the month, the time spent closing the books was cut by two days, and Wacoal now has real-time cash management instead of the once-a-day previous system. According to Hitachi's Nobuyuki Sambuichi:

> ❝ *The system significantly improves the quality of the financial data available to key decision makers. Since a major strength of XML is its ability to transform and transmit data from system to system regardless of the source, destination programs, or platforms, Wacoal's system can now provide up-to-date financial information to aid management decision-making. It also provides a fundamental real-time environment for gathering financial performance information from disparate systems such as purchasing, sales, materials, workflow, and inventory. Management can receive interim financial data, which gives them more time for analyzing results."* [261]

The system has liberated data within Wacoal: instead of the old approach that required an expert in part of the system to prepare a report, employees without special training can use standard queries and report writers.

As of this writing, seven years have passed since Wacoal implemented XBRL-GL, and despite the project's success, it's still the case study cited on XBRL groups' web site.[262] I find that astounding and disappointing. From my perspective, it appears that XBRL has become identified in the corporate mentality with regulatory compliance, blinding senior management to the wide array of ways in which it could be used strategically and profitably.

ENCHANTED OBJECTS

Let's look ahead to an entirely new kind of company that will be possible due to real-time sharing of structured data.

Two Boston-area firms that share the same ancestry, founder, and basic philosophy toward harnessing real-time data give us a glimpse of how a new kind of company will operate. Equally important, they preview how products capitalizing on ubiquitous real-time data will enrich our lives and even make us actually love data-driven objects, or, as these companies call them, "enchanted objects".

Ambient Devices and Vitality, Inc also illustrate a fascinating alternative version of data visualization, especially in light of the possibility that we will become overwhelmed by data if so much is available.

Based on what researchers call the "pre-attentive processing" phenomenon, the devices don't require that the user be specifically anticipating information or monitoring a display.[263]

Ambient Devices builds a range of devices based on that insight, which present the data in ways that provide constant awareness, but don't interrupt the user's routine or require that he or she stop everything and take some deliberate step to access the relevant information.

The devices are omnipresent (often located on a desk or night table) and powered by real-time public data such as National Weather Service forecasts or the stock market. They present that data in a variety of formats, some as simple as changing colors or sounds and neurological researchers say those subtle clues may be as or more valuable than the actual information in its original form, because they can provide a continuous information flow without demanding our full attention, as, for example, a numerical gauge might.

Take, for example, the Ambient Orb, a glass ball that glows in different colors to indicate changes in a variety of dynamic conditions: the stock market, weather, traffic, etc. Recently, Pacific Gas & Electric (PG&E) harnessed its power to improve customer compliance with conserving energy during high-demand periods. They introduced the PG&E Demand-Response Orb, which changes color when the utility sends out a signal that conservation is critical.[264]Ambient Devices encourages users to hack the Orb to display other data trends that are meaningful to them.[265]

ILLUSTRATION 6-6: THE AMBIENT ORB
source: Ambient Devices

However, the Ambient Devices product that I suspect is the most important harbinger of data-driven devices that will enrich our lives is its variation on a product that's about as plain vanilla as anything you can imagine, and was invented 4,000 years ago: the umbrella. Imagine that you live in rainy Seattle. When you come downstairs in the morning, your umbrella propped next to the front door is glowing, because its wireless receiver received a signal from Accu-Weather that it is going to rain or snow today![266]

If the 4,000-year-old umbrella can get an Internet of Things makeover, al-most *any* product, no matter how pedestrian, is fair game for being reinvented in a new way that harnesses real-time information. As more and more real-time data feeds become available from government or commercial sources, look for entre-preneurs to harness that information to create a wide range of Internet of Things products that will be driven by that data.

NOT YOUR GRANDMOTHER'S PILL JAR TOP

For example, Ambient Devices founder David Rose has since created another start-up. This one makes caps for prescription jars.

Oh.

But these aren't your grandmother's bottle caps. They approach the real-time data issue from the other end of the equation: data that originates from the user and then flows automatically to a wide range of uses.

Building on the same pre-attentive processing phenomenon that the Ambient De-vices products capitalize upon, the Vitality GlowCap attacks a major shortcoming in medical care that has never been addressed effectively by conventional means: the extremely high percent age of patients who fail to take their prescriptions on time. One-half of all adult Americans have some sort of prescription (that's 115 million people), but according to a study by the New England Health Institute, only about half of that group actually take their medications on time.[267]

This means that in the United States, over 57 million people aren't taking their prescriptions properly. That's a big problem, and a big potential market.

The problem is particularly acute for chronic conditions such as heart disease or diabetes: everyone loses when prescriptions aren't taken on time, or, even worse, not at all. The patient doesn't get needed medication, the doctor has no way of telling how much medication the patient actually took, the pharmaceutical manufacturer doesn't sell as many refills, and insurers end up paying for very expensive hospitalizations that might have been avoided. The New England Health Institute study reckons the total costs of non-compliance at $290 billion annually, an underappreciated major factor in soaring health care costs![268]

Building on The Orb model, the GlowCap replaces a conventional prescription container cap with one that includes a low-power wireless transmitter and a light. Because they are Internet of Things devices, each cap has its own IP address.

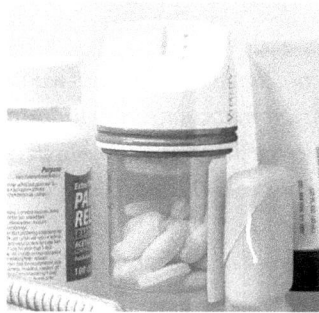

IMAGE 6-8: VITALITY GLOW CAP
Source: Vitality, Inc.

If you have one or more prescriptions, each of your GlowCaps is programmed with the time when you need to take that particular medication. When that time approaches, the GlowCap glows orange, as does the night light/base unit, which relays data to and from the Web. If more than an hour passes after the set time, it plays a ringtone as a further reminder to take the pill. After another hour, you get a reminder phone call. Rose says that to reinforce the message's importance, a future version may include your own doctor's voice making the reminder call.

When the cap is removed, that information is instantly transmitted to the base unit, and from there to the Web among other things, flowing directly to your medical record, so your doctor knows, in real time, if you took the pill.

Because data is at the heart of the system, it also can provide you and your doctor with weekly graphic reports on your level of compliance.

The bottom line? The on-time prescription use among those using the GlowCap increases dramatically, to 85%. The caps are marketed to those with the most at stake financially when patients don't take their prescriptions: the pharmaceutical companies and insurance plans.

One tech leader has predicted by 2020 there will be fifty billion Internet-of-Things connected devices,[269] but if I had to guess, I'd go with the wildly optimistic prediction of Linux Foundation Executive Director Jim Zemlin: two *trillion* web-connected devices in twenty years. As *The Economist* reported in a feature on the Internet of Things:

> ❝ *All that (achieving Zemlin's prediction) would require would be for everyone with an Internet connection today to have 1,000 of their possessions talking to the Internet. People in developed countries are reckoned to have between 1,000 and 5,000 possessions. Your correspondent has close on 1,000 books on his shelves, and many times that number of nuts, bolts, brackets and other bits in his garage."* [270]

Imagine the potential benefits in so many areas health care, energy, operating efficiency, and streamlining our lives that would become commonplace if this prediction is correct, and the boost that would provide to the economy.

CEMEX AND REAL-TIME DATA

Executives of old, established firms saddled with all sorts of redundant, sometimes conflicting, data reporting systems understandably roll their eyes when they read about start-ups such as Vitality, Inc. or about XBRL GL. "It's one thing to capitalize on instantaneous data sharing when you're starting from scratch today, but how can we possibly make that transition?"

The answer may lie in a company that's more than a century old, operates in perhaps the most backward industry in terms of communications, and is headquartered not in Silicon Valley but in Mexico.

Beginning in the 1990s, Cemex has consistently been a communications innovation leader, so much so that it is listed on *Wired* magazine's Wired 40,[271] with decisive leadership from CEO and Chairman Lorenzo H. Zambrano, grandson of the company's foundeIt's particularly interesting that Cemex is such a leader in real-time data sharing because it's in an industry where that's anything but the norm. In a 2007 article, attorney Barry LePatner detailed how "thousands of construction companies have resisted innovation and now survive as the last large mom-and-pop industry, and how that in turn leads to billions of dollars of waste every year,"[272] marked especially by poor communications between the companies. A major construction project such as Boston's much-maligned "Big Dig" highway project could be brought to a complete halt on a day when just one small, but critical, subcontractor failed to show up on time. For want of a load of cement a tunnel opening was delayed....

But Zambrano saw early on that advanced communications might give his company an edge in a commodity business, where there's little to distinguish competitors on an oops—bad pun—concrete basis.

When he took over the company, dispatching concrete trucks to construction sites was routinely done on the basis of schedules printed a day in advance. Never mind that clients would often cancel orders the day delivery was scheduled. You can imagine that this might well have been a defensible business practice: if you couldn't be sure of delivery, why not hedge your bets by over-ordering, then cancelling at the last minute?

Zambrano is not only a world leader in applied technology, but also in constantly fostering innovation within Cemex. So when he targeted communications as a critical target, he and then-CIO Kenneth Massey led a contingent of Cemex executives north of the border not to study leaders in the construction industry, but also organizations in other fields whose common denominator was similar to theirs:

needing to coordinate complex logistics in chaotic situations.

While visiting FedEx's dispatch center in Memphis was helpful, it was really the headquarters of Houston's EMT squad where Cemex learned the most. As Homero Saleh, who heads Cemex's Center for Business Processes told *Wired*'s Peter Katel:

> ❝ We wondered, 'How can they be dealing with emergencies?' The answer was that what was an emergency for us was routine for them. Lessons? The system got the necessary information from people quickly. It pinpointed available resources in real time. And it gave operators on the spot not distant managers the authority to respond instantly."[273]

Cemex began to rebuild the entire company around real-time data and the tools to capitalize on that data.

They linked all company facilities through a combination of public carriers and their own satellite system. In the 1990s, before most companies had heard of GPS, let alone implemented it, all of Cemex's cement trucks had built-in GPS units, with information relayed back to the dispatcher's office on a real-time basis. The dispatchers' displays let them see all trucks near a given customer's site, so they could dispatch the closest one.

Cemex also realized that the real potential of real-time data was realized only when two conditions were met: it was delivered to all those in the company who needed it, especially the dispatchers; and employees were empowered to use the data to make substantive decisions. The sophisticated tracking technology enabled the system, but it was giving dispatchers the power to act on data by re-routing trucks and changing production schedules that made it work.

The ability to speed delivery gave Cemex the chance to pioneer a new approach to both pricing and customer satisfaction. If the truck didn't reach the job site within twenty minutes of the customer's call, Cemex did a riff on another industry emphasizing speedy delivery (pizza shops), offering a discount of approximately twenty percent. Building on that reliability, Massey sold Zambrano on what he called "impeccability," where dispatchers could offer customers almost total satisfaction. Reliable deliveries soared to 95%, and they were within twenty minutes of promised delivery 90% of the time. [274]

All because of real-time data and ways to use it!

Equally important, Cemex eliminated data silos, and applied the same philosophy of real-time reporting to other data streams through what they called Dynamic Operation Synchronization (DOS). That means no one factor is considered in isolation, but in relationship to all the other ones that line workers and management must constantly consider. The dispatchers' dashboards (anticipating some of the more recent business intelligence dashboards) integrate displays of:

→ Orders by plant
→ Travels by truck
→ Distribution of demand timetable (by plant)
→ Order status

As a result, overall resource optimization increased by 28%, and team productivity increased 30%.[275]

Please excuse Humberto Zambrano if he laughs in your face when you say the concept of real-time data sharing is nice but not practical for you. Cemex had three strikes against it: in a commodity business, in a backward industry, and in a developing nation.

If Cemex could do it, can't you?

LIVING BY NUMBERS

Since the commercial introduction of barcodes in 1966, they've been a godsend to retailers and manufacturers, which use information from scanning the codes on items as they are distributed and purchased to improve logistics and to learn tremendous amounts about our buying habits

On the other hand, do you understand barcodes? What have they done for you?

Barcodes are yet another example of data that is very much a part of our daily lives and gets a lot of its power because of us (for example, what they show retailers about our personal buying patterns), but has given *consumers* little direct benefit, and remains largely a mystery to everyday people.

That's all changing now: just one example of how liberating data doesn't just improve government and business, but can have a profound impact on improving our daily lives, health, and satisfaction. It's our data, and we will decide how to use it.

PIC2SHOP

Pic2shop is a free iPhone app. When you photograph a barcode with your iPhone, it uploads the image to a site where the barcode is automatically linked to prices from other retailers, product reviews, etc., all accessible because they share the same metadata, with the barcode! That information, accessible in a usable form to you and me for the first time, empowers consumers. Some smart users now show a store manager their iPhone display and ask if the store will match the best price. Others may decide not to make an impulse buy because of reading a negative review of the product while standing in front of it in the store.

ILLUSTRATION 7-1: PIC2SHOP
source: pic2shop.com

With the pic2shop app and others like it, you and I are, for the first time, part of the club. This data is now at our command.

As this trend continues, we will all benefit:

➔ As real-time feedback allows monitoring our health conditions continuously, and improving our fitness by reinforcing new, healthy behaviors: what is being called "personal informatics" or the "quantified self".[276]

➔ Increasing the variety of location-based services that save time, cut needless driving, and (ironically for a web-based service) strengthen our ties to our own bricks-and-mortar communities.

➔ Helping us become smarter consumers by giving us information to choose more wisely and forcing retailers to provide us with that information if they want to compete for our attention.

➔ Helping us as individuals and groups improve our communities, nations, and planet by new initiatives that document environmental and other problems and our personal contributions toward their solution.

The combination of Web 2.0 devices and apps even create the exciting potential that we will no longer be just the passive recipients of data that's collected by government and industry about our lives.

Instead, we will also create the ultimate in democratized data: collecting, aggregating and evaluating ourselves data about important issues that businesses and government agencies either can't or won't collect but that still matters.

Three-way partnerships among government, business and people will become increasingly common and productive.

ACCESS TO DATA TRANSFORMING OUR DAILY LIFE

Let's look at a variety of examples of emerging services in two areas, location-based services (LBS) and comparison data, to sense what a transformation this personal access to data and the tools to use it is already beginning to create

As mentioned in Chapter 1, we've become so accustomed to GPS navigation devices in our cars and cell phones that it's hard to remember that before 2000, the government intentionally degraded the information from the twenty-four satellites that provide the data for these devices on the basis that it might be used by enemies to pinpoint targets for military or terrorist attacks.

The Clinton Administration was persuaded that the peaceful uses of accurate GPS data would more than counterbalance the threats, and in 1996 they began to gradually increase the accuracy of the signals for civilian use.

The government was right. The result has been a multi-billion dollar location-based services (LBS) industry that both creates entrepreneurial opportunities and improves users' lives.

In many ways, GPS-enabled LBS epitomizes both liberating data's potential and the need for creative governmental/business/consumer collaboration to fully capitalize on it:

➔ Funded by taxpayers, government provides the real-time data, and does so as a side-benefit of a critical national security program, at relatively little additional cost. As with other structured data, once it has been collected for one use, the data can also flow instantly to other uses.

→ Entrepreneurs and mainstream businesses and non-profit institutions create the mashups of the GPS data and other data that translate into valuable services to improve our lives.

→ Consumers buy and upgrade the increasingly powerful and versatile GPS-based devices that in turn allow more powerful applications to exploit that increased versatility.

→ The data flows automatically into devices without us having to do anything manually. They just operate dependably and in user-friendly ways that don't require special training on our part.

The result leverages all parties' resources for a mutually beneficial collaboration.

Liberating government data in general is likely to increase and diversify location-based services because government agencies have accumulated so much geospatial data in the recent past. Geospatial information is likely to be the easiest for agencies to release on a real-time basis and to be mashed up with other data to create valuable new services.

For example, in the United States, the largest portion of the first 100,000 data sets released on the Data.gov site were geospatial ones.[277] Given how specialized many of these are (and bearing in mind that government agencies don't just arbitrarily collect most of this data; they usually do so because the data has significant economic and/or social value), it's highly likely that both entrepreneurs and existing organizations with a strong stake in geographic information (natural resource extraction firms, logistics and transportation companies, etc. and/or environmental activists and other non-profits) will quickly develop applications to capitalize on them.

TRANSPORTATION

One part of our lives that will definitely benefit from the increase in real-time geospatial information will be all aspects of transportation.

There are few things more irritating than dutifully consulting the transit schedule, going to the bus stop or subway station at the correct time, and waiting for a bus or train that never arrives. Now riders of a number of subway systems, including the District of Columbia and San Francisco, can use smartphone apps to give them real-time transit information. Instead of waiting restlessly at the bus stop, they can stay in the comfort of their homes until just before the bus will actually arrive, or they can do errands nearby (a boon to local merchants) productively using waiting time that was previously wasted.

ILLUSTRATION 7-2: FIND A METRO STATION DC IPHONE APP
source: MARTA

Another application lets users access real-time FAA data on airplane arrivals.[278]

Perhaps most promising will be the advent of GPS devices that not only provide mapping but integrate real-time traffic data (perhaps not just from government-installed sensors and traffic cameras but also from the cars and trucks themselves or even Postal Service delivery vehicles[279] as more vehicles add sophisticated data broadcasting functions), then automatically generate alternative routes to steer around the congestion.

As more geospatial information becomes readily available (especially if it caters to the needs of specific niche groups), new mashups of that data will inevitably follow, including marketing-oriented ones. These location-based services are particularly valuable because they help change the balance of power between companies and the public: we are no longer tethered to our homes to read print ads or see

DATA DYNAMITE: How Liberating Information Will Transform Our World

TV commercials, and marketers will need to court us as we exploit this newfound consumer mobility. For example, they will need more targeted campaigns such as short-term discounts that only apply to (and will be seen by!) those who happen to be near a given store at a given time.

In addition, as smart businesses begin to realize how real-time data in our hands has given consumers new power, they will be forced to provide more of that information to be competitive, creating a virtuous loop in which more information begets more information. Even more dramatic, this real-time information availability may actually force companies to change their products and pricing, because we will be able to make instant comparisons between competing products, and become more discriminating and vocal consumers.

For example, Healthy and Fit Communities is a non-profit group that, as the name implies, wants to improve our eating habits. Its iPhone app, Restaurant Nutrition, lists the nutritional information for a wide range of fast-food restaurants.

Using Restaurant Nutrition, nutrition-conscious consumers can now start choosing which nearby fast-food restaurant to patronize on the basis of which has the most healthy menu items. That information in consumers' hands will increase pressure on the fast-food chains to reduce their saturated fat content and to provide more nutritional foods. All simply because we now have real-time information in our own hands.

ILLUSTRATION 7-3: RESTAURANT NUTRITION IPHONE APP
source: Healthy & Fit Communities

DATA ISN'T ENOUGH: THE TOOLS TO USE IT TRANSFORM THINGS

As vital as achieving access to real-time, structured data is, as we learned in Chapter 3, that data is of little use without applications and devices that can capitalize on it. That is particularly the case when individual use of data is concerned: most of us have neither the resources nor skills to interpret and use that data on our own, and it is of most value when we can access it when and where we need it to make decisions.

Perhaps nothing illustrates that as dramatically as the incredible increase in the number of applications for the iPhone since its introduction in June 2007, and the Android platform since it was introduced in November of that year. More than 300,000 iPhone apps and 200,000 Android apps exist as of this writing, many of which capitalize on integrating several smartphone features including the camera, the motion detector, and the built-in GPS, and the mashing-up of multiple data streams.

Ironically, some of these applications, while aimed at creating and enlarging virtual communities, may simultaneously strengthen our bricks-and-mortar communities as well. These apps can help you make new friends among those who frequent the same locations and share the same tastes, finding nearby vendors who sell products that you want, and/or giving tips on services and places to patronize or avoid.

For example, Foursquare combines a social networking application with location-based services. It lets you (among other things) share insider tips with your existing social network, as well as check in as you visit public places such as restaurants and stores. If you are the first person to have visited a venue, you can register it with Foursquare so others can also find it. If one of your friends who also uses Foursquare happens to be nearby at the time you check in, you can have an impromptu get-together. Perhaps the greatest value, however, is created when you leave a tip for other users about something you like or dislike about the place and its services. Realizing what a powerful marketing tool this could be, in early 2010 major publishers and other companies began signing multi-million dollar contracts with Foursquare,[280] and retailers such as Starbucks now offer special discounts, especially for the "mayor," which is Foursquare-speak for the most frequent visitor to a venue.

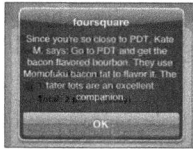

ILLUSTRATION 7-4: FOURSQUARE TIP
Source: Foursquare

REAL-TIME DATA WILL EMPOWER AMATEUR APP DEVEL-OPERS

As government agencies in the U.S. and elsewhere begin to release more high-value data streams under the Open Government Directive, the increase in applications for smartphones will accelerate. Many of them will be written not by professionals or with profit in mind, but by people with a real vision of the need for information or with a strong personal interest they want to share.

This is a subject of particular interest to me, because my own work in homeland security and disaster management convinces me that access to real-time information in an easy-to-use format can literally be a matter of life or death.

In fact, I used data to do something about the situation.

Just before the Iraq war began, there was a lot of fear the U.S. invasion might trigger another terrorist attack on the United States. I'd argued for several years that there should be apps for smartphones summarizing the best information to help individuals prepare for, or respond to, a natural disaster or terrorist attack. If there were such apps, at least some people would be able to take care of themselves and others nearby, lessening the burden on first responders by referring to the advice in the program.[281] The idea got lots of praise, but no one actually took it on.

Given the level of concern about preparedness, in 2003 I decided to do what I'd urged others to do. I quickly analyzed and prioritized all the best sources of information on the issue, not only from the US but also the UK, Israel, and other countries that had a lot of experience dealing with terrorists. The result was the "Terrorism Survival Planner," an app that would allow the user, in only three clicks, to go from a top-level category (such as "evacuation" or "communication") to detailed information about what to do.

IMAGE 7-5: TERRORISM SURVIVAL PLANNER
source: Stephenson Strategies & Town Compass

While the program received a lot of critical acclaim,[282] it was simply too time consuming for me to continue to update it, so I eventually had to pull it from circulation.

However, if the data that I had to manually cut and paste into the app was instead available as real-time data feeds, and I had designed the app to accept structured data, then every time a user synched his or her smartphone, it would be automatically updated without further effort. I still hope that the Department of Homeland Security will someday listen to me and authorize such data streams.

Millions of people, each with their own concern and area of expertise gardening, cooking, or caring for an aging relative could and would design similar programs if the needed data was available, combined with simple tools to work with it.

COMPARISON INFORMATION

Another important way in which release of real-time structured information will improve our daily lives is in being able to compare products and services in an apples-to-apples context.

That was the thinking behind the Security and Exchange Commission's decision to require publicly traded companies to report using XBRL: beginning in 2012, the

Commission will publish data for these firms using the XBRL tags, which will mean that for the first time it will be possible to make an apples-to-apples comparison between two stocks. You already benefit from this phenomenon when you go to the Google Products Search site or other comparison shopping sites. Companies have learned that if they want their products displayed on the site, they must tag important data about the product such as model number, price, sizes, shipping weight, so that the page's search algorithm will include their product in the comparison. There is positive pressure to get with the program: use your own idiosyncratic terms and you'll be punished by the marketplace!

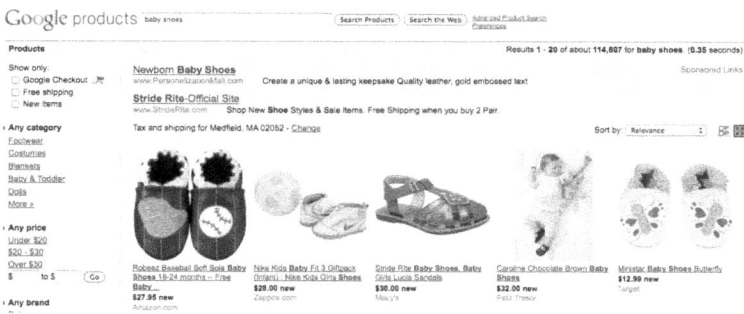

ILLUSTRATION 7-6: GOOGLE PRODUCT SEARCH
source: Google

When he announced the SEC's initiative to require publicly traded firms to file mandated reports in XBRL formats, SEC chair Christopher Cox said that one of the reasons for the change was that corporate information was previously buried in SEC documents; now, "if it is appropriately inputted [ie., using XBRL], it can be mixed and matched in an infinite variety of ways" to help analysts and investors make exact, direct comparisons between various companies' financial data.[283]

In addition, a variety of data that government has compiled in the past as part of qualitative analysis of health care and other services can help us make more informed decisions as health-care consumers. For example, the Medicare Hospital Quality Compare website takes data from patient surveys regarding recent hospital stays and then allows users to compare quality of care regarding various medical conditions or surgical procedures. As more structured data from government and corporate data bases becomes available, it is likely that a growing number of consumer groups and activists will create similar websites allowing similar head-to-head comparisons that will improve users' ability to make informed decisions.[284]

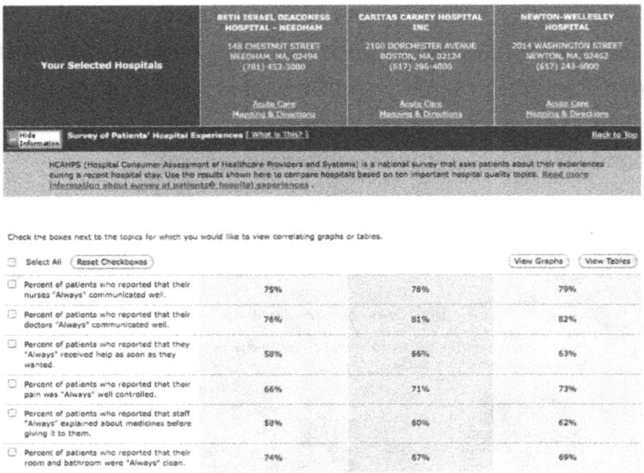

ILLUSTRATION 7-7: MEDICARE HOSPITAL QUALITY COMPARE COMPARISONS OF THREE HOSPITALS
source: Medicare Hospital Quality Compare website

DATA OF THE PEOPLE, BY THE PEOPLE, AND FOR THE PEOPLE

Most of *Data Dynamite* focuses on making data available to us that government and industry compile from our demographic patterns, our purchasing, and other aspects of our lives, whether at work or in public.

That's vital, because of the vast stores of such data already in existence and because we should have access to information about us that others are able to use but we are not.

However, there is another increasingly important aspect of liberating data that has been made possible by recent advances, especially in mobile computing and social applications.

This is data that we, the people, actually generate and control from the beginning.

It is data that can directly improve our lives, help us change our habits for the better, and even empower our virtual and concrete communities.

It is data that we record as part of daily living and then analyze either individually or collectively using the data visualization and collaboration tools mentioned in Chapter 3.

The concept predates modern technology.[285] Since 1900, the National Audubon Society has conducted an annual "Christmas Bird Count", in which volunteers observe and report the number of each species of birds near their homes. The first year, 27 volunteers counted 18,500 individual birds representing 90 species on Christmas Day.[286] By 2009, the event covered the Americas, ran from December 14 through January 5, 2010, and was labeled "Citizen Science In Action." The totals? 1,729 counts and 51,735,873 birds. [287] Over the years, the changes and patterns in the counts have been credited with leading to new environmental regulations and protection for species such as the American Black Duck.[288]

Statistical reporting by individuals has moved to a higher level with the introduction of new personal communication devices and Web 2.0 apps.

Several years ago, after adventurer Steve Fossett's small plane went down, I helped in the search for the wreckage. How did I do this? In my bed, early in the morning, and while simultaneously eating breakfast and watching CNN.

Like many, I'd been intrigued by an article saying that Fawcett's friend Richard Branson was footing the bill to use Amazon's Mechanical Turk service to aid in the search. [289] In less than fifteen minutes I'd found the website, signed up, and had been assigned several map quadrants to analyze to see if they might include anything resembling plane wreckage (there was a reference photo of an actual crash of a similar plane to use for comparison).

That was my introduction to how powerful it can be when large numbers of individuals come together virtually, linked by increasingly powerful collaboration tools, to address a common problem. In recent years the phenomenon has taken a new twist: virtual groups of interested individuals are not just interpreting data but actually gathering it themselves.

The phenomenon goes by many names, but I like Yale astronomer Kevin Schawinski's term, "citizen science". Contrasting it to the crowd-sourcing concept, Schawinski says this approach has more rigor: "You're a regular citizen but you're doing science. Crowdsourcing sounds a bit like, well, you're just a member of the crowd, and you're not: you're our collaborator. You're proactively involved in the process of science by participating".[290]

Schawinski should know. In 2007, while a grad student at Oxford, he faced a daunting task that somewhat paralleled the search for Steve Fawcett's plane: he needed to analyze 50,000 images of galaxies and classify them in terms of whether they were spiral or elliptical shaped. Overwhelmed, he brainstormed with a pub mate what to do, and came up with Galaxy Zoo, a citizen science project where volunteers were asked to analyze and classify the images. Because of a BBC show hosted by his beer-drinking buddy, thousands signed up when the project launched in 2007. The server became so overloaded by the volunteer analysts that a cable melted.

Within the first year and a half, the number of users increased to 180,000, and they had classified one million different images (Schawinski estimates it would have taken him 124 years to have achieved the same results working by himself!). Interestingly, the astronomer found that his original qualms about trusting amateurs to do the analysis were unwarranted: in reality they may actually be better than professionals in these tasks because they don't have the same preconceptions about what they're seeing.[291] The Buddhist' "beginner's mind" concept in practice!

Galaxy Zoo isn't just an imaging analysis process: participants have made some significant discoveries. University of Alabama Professor Bill Keel asked them to notify him if they found examples of the rare phenomenon of overlapping galaxies. More than one hundred participants reported such findings in the first day, and thousands have been seen since then. Schawinski was also surprised at just how many people are interested in donating time to the project, noting that users range from individuals with no astronomy background to school teachers and students to parents who participate with their children as a sort of family activity. Dutch teacher Hanny van Arkel, another Galaxy Zoo enthusiast, found "Hanny's Voorwerp," a dust cloud illuminated by a nearby quasar, and Schawinski credits van Arkel's judgment as being the key: "Computers cannot recognize the unusual. Humans can."[292]

Beyond having individuals analyze data collected by high-resolution electron telescopes, the citizen science phenomenon also includes projects where people actually gather the information themselves.

The natural sciences are particularly fertile ground for citizen scientists, because field studies of migration paths, inventories of habitats and other dispersed measurements are so important to the science. For example, projects highlighted in the Citizen Science blog include ones where participants take daily UV radiation readings and compare them with predicted readings from weather services and there is the Great Sunflower Project, which attempts to learn about bees' health by recording whether they visit sunflowers grown from specific wild sunflower seeds.[293]

Perhaps the most exciting vision of citizen science's future potential is offered by the EpiCollect app for the Android and iPhone smartphones, because it combines all of the cutting-edge technologies that make real-time data collection and analysis possible for the first time. It was developed for professional scientists doing field work in epidemiology and ecology, but can also be used by lay people.

EpiCollect takes advantage of the phone's GPS unit in combination with Google Maps, automatically geo-locating the observations, a necessity for precise fieldwork that in the past was difficult and time consuming even for professionals. EpiCollect lets the user input data directly into a web-based database, which then instantly analyzes the information and plots it in real-time on maps, so that the researchers can begin to detect patterns in their observations while still in the field, rather than having to later enter data back at the lab. They can also attach photos from the phone's camera.

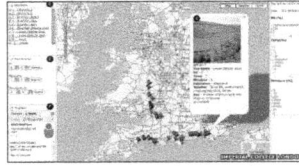

David Aanenen of Imperial College in London, the lead researcher, told the BBC that the system could be particularly valuable for involving students in research by having kids study the number of species in a specific area and then compare the results with other schools, even ones in other countries.[294]

VOLUNTEERING YOUR DEVICE

Citizens can also use the combination of powerful mobile devices and social media apps to provide invaluable data in crisis situations.

This is a subject that's particularly near and dear to my heart, because it's at the core of the "networked homeland security" theory that I have developed since 9/11.[295]

It began when I wrote a Boston *Globe* op-ed weeks after the tragedy, in which I suggested a number of ways in which web-based tools could be used to fight terror. Out of all of the ideas, the *Globe* headline writer chose to highlight use of handhelds, titling it "Fighting Terror With Palm Pilots".[296]

At that time, given the laughably limited power of handhelds as compared to today (particularly the lack of GPS and camera functions), I suggested the main value of the handhelds was to hold previously downloaded disaster response instructions that people could use to be self-directed if all communications was disrupted in a terror attack. If even one person in a group had the program, he or she could share the information and increase the chances that at least some people would be able to take care of themselves.[297] That lead to the Terrorism Survival Planner mentioned earlier.

As handhelds added new functions and new applications were developed to capitalize on those features, I expanded the vision of how you and I could be critical players in response to a terror attack.[298] I point out that because using programs such as Twitter and Facebook on handhelds have become second nature in our daily lives, we'll probably use them automatically in disasters as well, whether officials want us to or not.

So, I argue, if that's the case, officials should capitalize on the inevitable, and figure out how to maximize the benefit of such information (and, because bad guys have cell phones too, minimize the problems with deceptive information), and then create formal programs both to educate us on how best capitalize on these devices to provide valuable, real-time situational awareness to officials, and to incorporate the social media in their formal emergency communication programs.

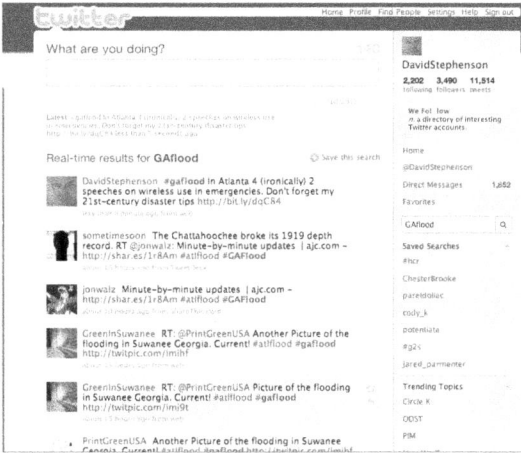

ILLUSTRATION 7-9: TWEETS DURING THE SEPTEMBER 2009 GEORGIA FLOODS
source: Twitter

In particular, I have suggested that officials need to provide instruction for the public on how to use the phone's camera and/or video functions to document disaster situations, since a photo or video can provide such a wealth of information (and, if the video is uploaded to a site such as Twitvid it is automatically tagged with geolocation data, making it even more valuable). Since there are more of "us" than there are of first responders, it's likely that you or I may be the first to happen on the scene of a disaster or terrorist attack, and that we could provided invaluable situational awareness to authorities.

The most exciting example to date of an effort to formally channel social media during disasters was developed in the wake of the 2010 Haitian earthquake by Project EPIC (Empowering the Public with Information In Crisis). Consistent with liberating data principles, they developed a series of "hashtags," (#location, #status, #needs, #damage) to preface tweets, so that information following the hashtags could be easily machine-readable and therefore spread and analyzed automatically. This is a phenomenal example of the power of social media combined with structured data. Who would have believed that it would be possible to provide substantive, actionable, real-time situational awareness in only 140 characters (that economy, incidentally, could be critical in a crisis, when bandwidth is reduced).[299]

Sample Before & After Tweet Makeovers:

TWEET-BEFORE: roads from PAP to les Cayes are open migration from PAP to rural areas has begun
TWEET-AFTER: #haiti #open roads from #loc PAP to les Cayes are open #info migration from PAP to rural areas has begun
This tells the computer:
what = road
what about it = open
where = at PaP to les Cayes
what else: "open migration from PAP to rural areas has begun"

. . . .

ILLUSTRATION 7-10: TWEET FROM HAITI USING "TWEEK THE TWEET" HASHTAGS
source: Project EPIC

Another cutting-edge example of crowdsourcing of data using personal communication devices and Web 2.0 applications is the phenomenon of augmented reality.

You may be familiar with a glitzy version of augmented reality, when computer-generated first-down lines are superimposed over an actual football field. Now the same approach is being used on a grassroots level, particularly to augment streetscapes with audio and/or video information concerning issues such as historical notes or personal observations that is superimposed over a picture of a given building. For example, when touring Atlanta's historic Oakland Cemetery, the

DATA DYNAMITE: How Liberating Information Will Transform Our World

"Voices of Oakland" project allows visitors wearing headsets and carrying laptops to "hear" the voices of prominent citizens buried there.[300]

ILLUSTRATION 7-11: AUGMENTED REALITY VIEW OF PIAZZA RIFORMA, LUGANO, WITH INFORMATION SUPERIMPOSED

A particularly exciting project is capitalizing on the technology so that European tourists will be able to visualize historic buildings that have vanished or decayed over time. When you focus your smartphone camera on an object, the iTacitus shows additional information, and can even help you organize a sightseeing trip based on which interests you check in a survey using the app.[301] As augmented reality tools become more ubiquitous, it is likely that volunteers will take it upon themselves to annotate streetscapes, natural vistas and other locations to enhance sightseeing and/or share information about stores and other venues.

THE EXAMINED LIFE IS WORTH LIVING

Liberating data on the personal level won't just make us better informed, it will help us change our lives, by making us data conscious and helping us to interpret how that data can help us to eliminate bad habits and create beneficial new ones, whether they affect our personal health or the planet's.

One of the leaders of this new movement, sometimes referred to as the "Quantified Self", is Kevin Kelly, founding editor of *Wired*, and a paradigm buster since his early years on the staff of the *Whole Earth Catalogue*. Kelly is one of several authors of the blog *Quantified Self*, and has summarized this concept of data as a driver for personal change: "Unless something can be measured, it cannot be improved…So we are on a quest to collect as many personal tools that will assist us in quantifiable measurement of ourselves. We welcome tools that help us see and understand bodies and minds so that we can figure out what humans are here for."

ENVIRONMENTAL

Reducing global warming will demand both massive governmental intervention and personal habit change.

To help you reduce your own carbon footprint303 as well as your general environmental impacts and your risk from environmental hazards, the online Personal Environmental Impact Report (PEIR) interacts with your mobile phone to give you an environmental "scorecard" that tracks some of your effects on the environment and some of what you are exposed to daily.

PEIR is reminiscent of the TIES emergency management dashboard described in Chapter 3 because it brings together so many real-time, location-based data sources.[304] For example, each user has their own PEIR profile which combines daily, weekly, monthly and yearly summaries of your:

→ Carbon emissions
→ Impact on sensitive sites such as schools and hospitals where poor air quality increases risk
→ Fast-food exposure
→ Particulate exposure

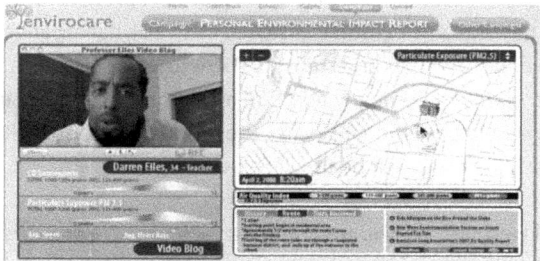

ILLUSTRATION 7-12: PEIR DISPLAY, COMBINING LIVE VIDEO, STATISTICS & MAPPING
source: PEIR project

You can also share your overall PEIR scores with other users or add a widget to Facebook (students from several San Francisco high schools are using the social function to stage a win-win competition to see who can reduce their impact the most).

HEALTH AND FITNESS

The Nike+ is a small chip that you insert into a pocket in Nike+ enabled shoes, which then tracks the length and speed of your run plus the calories burned. At the end of the run you upload the results to their website (it will come as no surprise to you the data is structured using XML so it can be read by a number of programs). The data is turned into a variety of visually compelling charts to not only track your results but to motivate you in the future. The site has become "the largest community of runners ever assembled—more than 1.2 million runners who have collectively tracked more than 130 million miles and burned more than 13 billion calories".[305]

The site has proven a goldmine for medical and behavioral analysts. One surprising finding that underscores the value of data visualization is that Nike has discovered that there's a magic number for a Nike+ user: five. If someone uploads two or three runs to the site, they're probably trying it out. But once they enter five runs, they're much more likely to keep running and uploading data. At five runs, they've gotten hooked on what their data tells them about themselves."[306]

South Korea recently announced that it will launch a program using 3G applications to help patients with chronic diseases that will have patients input their glucose meter measurements and transmit them to Korea Telecom's u-Health Platform. The glucose meter company and Korea Telecom will create software to link hospital medical data bases and u-Health. The program will also include content to help the patients improve their health lifestyles.[307]

New apps and web sites to help people track their exercise regimes and diet crop up daily, all exploiting the power of data visualization as a motivator.

WHEN YOUR DATA IS A MATTER OF LIFE OR DEATH

As in several other chapters, I'll conclude this one with two examples where individuals' commitment to effective use of data involves serious illness and/or may be a matter of life or death.

In the 1990s, Alexandra Carmichael and her husband Daniel Reda had co-founded Redasoft, which specialized in visualization of complex genetic information, so they were well versed in the power of visual displays of medical information.

Carmichael, after more than a decade of unexplained, debilitating pelvic pain, was ultimately diagnosed by a homeopath with vulvodynia, a condition in which pain or irritation around the opening of the vulva is so intense it may be uncomfortable to sit or have sex. In 2008, the couple created CureTogether.com to "help people anonymously track and compare health data, to better understand their bodies, make more informed treatment decisions and contribute data to research."

She said her motivation for starting CureTogether was that "each patient has so much information in their body, but when you go to your doctor's you can't talk to all of those patients, so you have to go online".[308] The group originally dealt with vulvodynia, migraines, and endometriosis, but quickly expanded, so that patients dealing with more than 270 conditions were sharing information at the time of publication.

Using visual tools, participants may:

→ Track their symptoms over time, and see how they are similar or different from others with the same condition.

→ Compare what treatments others with similar conditions are receiving and how effective they are

→ Chart their weight, diet and other personal characteristics and correlate them with their treatments or dietary changes to see how their bodies are responding

→ Learn how to run experiments on themselves to see what effect new treatments or dietary changes are having on their bodies.

→ Network with others who have the same or similar conditions to learn from their experiences and make better treatment choices.

ILLUSTRATION 7-13: PERSONAL PROFILE PAGE ON CURETOGETHER
source: CureTogether.com

Carmichael has personally gone beyond just sharing on CureTogether. She tracks more than forty personal markers, from her diet to her sex life, a discipline that she sees as eventually leading to an era of *personalized medicine.* "I want to go to a site and enter all of my symptoms, my conditions, my biomarkers, my genetics every-thing about my body and it would tell me what treatment is most likely to work for me and with the fewest side effects."[309]

If CureTogether makes chronic illnesses more tolerable, PatientsLikeMe.com raises the stakes, focusing on people dealing with life-threatening illnesses, including amyotrophic lateral sclerosis (ALS), Parkinson's disease, HIV/AIDS, multiple sclerosis, and mood disorders.

Ben and James Heywood, two brothers in the high-tech field, and their friend Jeff Cole founded PatientsLikeMe after a third Heywood brother, Stephen, died of ALS.[310] Their goal is "to enable people to share information that can improve the lives of patients diagnosed with life-changing diseases".

PatientsLikeMe works by having patients post detailed information on their conditions on the site, where that data is anomizing and sold to medical device, drug, and insurance companies. The company aims to create the "largest repository of real-world disease information to help accelerate the discovery of new, more effective treatments".

The result is a win-win. Patients say that it breaks down the isolation they often feel and that they can learn from other patients' experience. The corporate sponsors gain access to data that helps researchers learn how these diseases act in the real world.

LIBERATING DATA WILL MOST AFFECT OUR DAILY LIVES

Liberating data will undoubtedly transform government and business, as we have already seen. However, it is likely that the transformation will be most dramatic and most profound when it comes to our daily lives, if for no other reason than that it is in that area that we have been most bereft of data in the past. The likely results will include better decision-making, support for our personal self-improvement goals, and harnessing our individual efforts and insights for the common good.

It is also likely, that, as toolkits are created that allow individuals with no background in programming to create apps themselves, the number and variety of apps to gather, report and analyze data aimed at individuals will radically increase. It will be driven by the diversity of interests, talents, and concerns of the billions of people worldwide who will be empowered by liberating data to use for themselves and the common good.

THE GLOBAL DATA-CENTRIC FUTURE

Beware of anyone who dares predict liberating data's future!

That's because of a miraculous phenomenon that we saw demonstrated in the earliest stage of this revolution. When the District of Columbia said that entrants in its pioneering Apps for Democracy contest could use any of the 270 data sets in its Citywide Data Warehouse, the contestants came up with more than forty usable apps, covering everything from real-time transit times to crowd-sourced historic tours.[311]

The lesson? Give ordinary people, whether inside or outside an organization, access to data and the means to interpret and work with it, and the variety in creative uses of that data will be unfathomable, simply because we humans are so varied in our individual interests, skills, and backgrounds. Five people with access to the same data will find five different ways to use it and that's before they mash it up with three other random data streams!

Equally important, as we have already seen in many cases, others, perhaps half a world away, will observe those uses and have "a-ha moments" in which they will think of ways to use another data set that addresses one of their concerns. The result will be synergy upon synergy and virtuous imitation that feeds upon itself and accelerates over time.

In short, the only thing we *can* predict about the future of liberating data is that we *cannot* predict the future of liberating data.

Chapter 1 cited some staggering statistics (particularly given the sixteenth century's communications limits) about how rapidly Luther's work spread throughout Europe and how it spawned a dramatic expansion of the number of books and pamphlets published.

There's every reason to believe that liberating data will have a similar impact. Like Luther, it will spur a revolution.

Why?

Both revolutions transfer power to the masses, taking away the priesthood's special role (in the case of data, the "priests" are statisticians, analysts, and senior management) in controlling access to information and the ability to determine how it was used. The Web is the twenty-first century version of the sixteenth century's printing press, but with one critical advantage: it is worldwide, transcending national boundaries and allowing not only global sharing of data, but also sharing of ideas on how to capitalize on it. Also, instead of many different alphabets and languages, we are moving toward global standards on data that will allow its global exchange and use.

Liberating data accelerated dramatically during the last few years, partially because of President Obama's public embrace of the concept, as manifested primarily by the launch of Data.gov and the Open Government Directive and other elements of his administration's transparency initiatives.

But Obama wasn't the catalyst: simply an accelerant, because so many people and organizations worldwide have embraced the cause. Without his initiatives, liberating data would have been only slightly delayed, for this is truly a global phenomenon. Those nations, companies, or individuals with few resources can still be leaders because the commitment to open source tools and global standards that are the movement's hallmarks mean there are no barriers to entry: the only requirements are commitment and ingenuity.

From the Dutch Taxonomy Project, to the UK government's creation of Data.gov.uk, to Vancouver's new open data pledge, to Netflix's crowd-sourcing of ideas for corporations, to the "Quantified Self" phenomenon of self-reporting of personal statistics, it is clear: the liberating data movement is robust and self-sustaining.

WHY THE TREND WILL ACCELERATE

If we cannot predict specifics about liberating data's future, we *can* look for indicators as to why it will continue to grow.

First, there is a *de facto* standard emerging that open source tools should be the cornerstone of efforts to capitalize on liberated data. That will make it simpler for those who join the movement later to quickly gain speed and offer robust programs. As amply demonstrated by what Dustin Haisler has accomplished in cash-strapped Manor, Texas, it will empower those who cannot afford expensive programming tools. What does Manor know that big cities do not? The District of Columbia's pioneering Apps for Democracy program required that the applications submitted to the contest be written in open source code, making it simple to copy and/or improve upon them. That contest also drove home the point by putting an explicit link to the code to make it easy to examine and copy. That decision stimulated a growing number of similar competitions around the world, all using variations on the same principles of sharing.

The fact that the United States' Data.gov program expanded from forty data sets in mid-May of 2009 to 100,000 by July of that year showed that it is likely many agencies and companies around the world already have data streams that can be released easily and at little cost, explaining why other nations quickly follow suit with their own data releases.

The Dutch Taxonomy Project (now Standard Business Reporting) model of a system that benefits government and businesses alike by allowing companies to file a single XBRL file rather than an array of traditional reports to a wide range of agencies has already inspired the governments of Australia and New Zealand to follow suit. As soon as a few more nations follow suit, multi-national companies will see that they could really benefit from a global reporting standard, and push for its adoption worldwide. When that happens, as the name implies, it really will be the standard for business reporting! When that happens, companies that are spending to have their data tagged with XBRL to report to government agencies will also come to realize they can amortize their expenses and gain many other benefits by bringing the tagging process into their daily operations by using XBRL GL instead of adding those tags at the end of the process, thereby streamlining their own operations and better integrating with their supply chain and customers.

Soaring government deficits worldwide because of massive spending necessary to lift the global economy out of the recession of 2008 have led to demands on both the right and left for greater transparency and accountability, while smart governments will come to realize they can eke more out of remaining budgets through more efficient operation.

As more highly respected companies such as Netflix crowdsource innovation by releasing more corporate data publicly, other companies will follow suit and be surprised by the benefits.

Finally, as formal or *ad hoc* grassroots groups such as CureTogether.com or the Nike+ users' group proliferate and as more apps such as pic2shop demonstrate how data can directly improve our daily lives, liberating data will become a part of everyone's experience, as was the democratization of printed materials in Luther's day. The barriers to entry are non-existent, while the benefits are far reaching.

While there will likely be obstacles along the way, there is simply an historical inevitability about making data readily available and universally usable for the common good.

THE SEMANTIC WEB WILL ACCELERATE TREND

Perhaps the most important overall factor driving liberating data in the near future will be the full implementation of Semantic Web technologies, if for no other reason than that they get such heavy media coverage thanks to Sir Tim Berners-Lee, the creator of the World Wide Web, who also created the Semantic Web concept, and pushes the concept so relentlessly.

If you haven't heard of the Semantic Web, it refers to a third-generation Web (in fact, the Semantic Web is often referred to as Web 3.0) in which (among other things) the Internet of Things will become ubiquitous, and computers and embedded devices will take over much of the labor of searching the Web. Instead of web pages just designed to be read by people, their content will also be designed to be read by machines. That, however, can't take place without tagged data, because computers can't deal with ambiguous instructions.[312] Berners-Lee refers to it as a "Web of data".[313]

To make the Semantic Web possible, not only pages will have http names: individual data items will as well, what are called Uniform Resource Identifiers (URIs), which have replaced the old Uniform Resource Locators (URLs) of the early days of the Web. Equally important, the data not just be whole Web pages – the data in those pages will be able to be linked separately. You can imagine that when this Web of data concept becomes commonplace, the demand for structured data will soar, which will in turn lead to demands that more of the data that organizations have stored should be shared.

Understandably, since Berners-Lee is an official advisor to Data.uk.gov, that site features a large amount of "linked data" specifically designed for Semantic Web, and Data.gov in the U.S. is doing the same.

That omnipresent data will drastically increase the potential mix-and-match potential of data as well as the benefits of using it.

BIG DATA

If the benefits of liberating your data aren't already compelling enough motivation for change, be forewarned that the Semantic Web and the Internet of Things is about ready to overwhelm you with data, both from inside and outside your organization.

The phenomenon is called Big Data. It is already here in limited venues (Walmart, for example, processes more than a million customer transactions every hour, feeding into databases totaling more than 2.5 petabytes[314]) and is about to become ubiquitous. That's because RFID chips, remote sensors, etc. will be found everywhere, and they will be feeding staggering amounts of data on a streaming, real-time basis (more than we can actually assimilate at this time: according to *The Economist*, in 2007 the amount of data generated surpassed the memory to store it[315]). Also, small and medium-sized companies will be able to take part in Big Data projects because the data can be stored online in the cloud, and free apps such as Hadoop can manage the data. Analyzing these huge data sets can lead to valuable insights into crime patterns, drug research, and business trends, so we must come up with effective means to manage and capitalize on them. Ironically, there's going to be so much data that it will increasingly be inaccessible by conventional means, according to Johns Hopkins Astrophysicist Alex Szalay.[3]

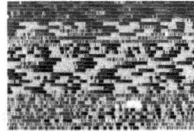

ILLUSTRATION 8-1: CHROMOGRAM VISUALIZATION OF COMMENTS BY WIKIPEDIA USER317
source: IBM

One of the issues is that these volumes of data exceed the power of conventional management tools to analyze them. Thus tools such as data visualizations, which abstract certain properties of the data and represent them through various colors or other symbolic means as a way of discerning meaning in the data, will become more and more important.

Big Data inevitably raises the question of whether we can ever have too much data. I suspect the answer is no: we may have too much data for conventional analysis and storage, but I suspect that the promise of being able to do real-time analytics and address major issues such as developing drugs aimed at specific parts of genetic code will mean that we will simply have to develop new management strategies and tools.

WHAT IF YOU LIBERATED DATA AND NOBODY CAME?

One of the potential dangers with the massive release of government and corporate databases worldwide is that those of us who are not trained statisticians will be overwhelmed by the volume of data and won't use it productively.

Similarly, some have estimated that up to 85% of all data is unstructured,[318] which threatens to overwhelm our human capacity to process unless, as I believe, people over time learn to think more in terms of structuring data *from the beginning*, thereby changing this ratio.[319]

Equally important, many of us don't understand the scientific principles behind data analysis, so we are likely to misinterpret data.

Thus, a critical step if liberating data is to make us data literate, just as the European masses gradually became literate in the years after Luther made the printed word easily available.

A necessary pre-condition to data literacy is making it seem more relevant and accessible to the general public. Many Eyes does that with its free data hosting and visualization tools, but governments and businesses alike must begin to host not only data sets, but also easy-to-use tools with which to use it.

Forum One Communications provided one step toward broad public use of data with its Datamasher tool, which won first prize in the Apps for America competition sponsored by the Sunlight Foundation to promote use of the Data.gov data sets.[320] Datamasher makes it simple for anyone to create a visualization comparing state-by-state results when two of the Data.gov data streams are combined in a mashup.

ILLUSTRATION 8-2: TYPICAL DATAMASHER MASHUP
source: DataMasher.com

According to company owner Chris Wolz, "We think that allowing people to explore government data in this way will get more people interested in learning about and using data produced by the government."[321] Yes, that includes having fun with the tool. Wolz himself produced one politically incorrect mashup, "Dumb Guns," which showed a strong *inverse* relationship (but not necessarily causality, I must add!) between rates of statewide handgun ownership and high-school graduation rates.

WHAT WILL BE POSSIBLE THAT IS NOW IMPOSSIBLE?

Icosystem CEO and chief scientist Eric Bonabeau launched me on the path that resulted in this book when he introduced me to the wonders of data visualization.

Last year he challenged me to make certain that *Data Dynamite* would explain how liberating data would make "possible what was impossible before". It seems fitting to conclude with a vision of what will be possible when we liberate data, to inspire each of you to take up the challenge.

On the surface, making data available and usable seems like something that would only matter to statisticians, but the breadth and profundity of change this will make possible is breathtaking:

PERSONAL

Patients will be able to band together for mutual support and knowledge supported by data, which will simultaneously and seamlessly provide researchers with a wealth of knowledge about real-life experiences that should speed drug and treatment options.

People concerned about environmental issues and how they may help in the face of such overwhelming challenges will be able to quantify their environmental impacts and track their own and society's progress toward change.

Consumers will become more informed and will demand and receive more information from sellers to help them compare products and prices.

Through personal metrics, individuals will gain valuable insights into their personal habits and their impacts and receive support for change.

A growing array of services based on real-time, location-based information will simplify our lives and use virtual world tools to strengthen our physical communities.

GOVERNMENT

Agencies will be able to deliver more services at lower cost because of unified, simplified reporting processes.

Agencies will improve their analysis and decision making by treating all workers as knowledge workers, and giving them access to the real-time data they need to make decisions.

Regulation will improve while reducing companies' reporting costs, because companies will file a single structured data file that all agencies can simultaneously access.

Agencies will be able to partner with the public to provide important new data-driven services at little or no cost: government provides the data, and individuals and companies turn it into valuable services.

Controversial programs will build public trust through unprecedented transparency, real-time reporting.

BUSINESS

Companies will be able to reduce their operating costs through just-in-time logistics and other innovations made possible through global standards for data sharing and real-time data.

They will improve their data analysis and decision-making because they will be able to give workers access to real-time, actionable data and the tools to use it.

They will need to develop new marketing methods, provide customers with more information, and even improve their products to compete for the new, empowered and informed customers.

They will earn public trust, destroyed by so many corporate transgressions in the recent past, through a "don't trust us, track us" approach based on data transparency.

These are only a few foreseeable benefits of liberating data. In reality, as people become more familiar with how to work with real-time, actionable data, and as amount and variety of generally-available data increases, it is highly likely that we will see whole new classes of data-driven devices, beneficial mashups of mix-and-match data, and innovations we can't yet conceive.

"... EACH MAN BECAME EAGER FOR KNOWLEDGE"

In 1542, German historian Johann Sleidan wrote:

" *…there was invented in our land a marvelous new and subtle art, the art of printing. This opened German eyes even as it is now bringing enlightenment to other countries. Each man became eager for knowledge, not without feeling a sense of amazement at all his former blindness."*[322]

Now we have our own marvelous (although by no means subtle!) invention, the Web. We find ourselves at what could prove to be every bit as dramatic an inflection point as the birth of empowering the ordinary individual to deal with the written word: the dawning of the age of liberated data.

We too should be eager for knowledge as we explore this unknown territory.

And, someday, we too may look back with a sense of amazement at how blind we had been -- to the power of data to create true democracy, global wealth, and personal growth.

I'm excited. How about you?

ACCELERATING DATA LIBERATION:
A MANIFESTO

Martin Luther's role in history would have been secure if he'd simply translated the Bible into German and printed it. However, he wasn't content with that. Luther directly challenged the status quo and the establishment with the 95 Theses that he tacked on the Wittenberg minster.[323]

While taking pains to stress that I don't see them rising to the importance of Luther's Theses[324] as a Liberating Data Manifesto, as it were, that will continue to be valid even if the underlying technologies change dramatically, as they surely will.

Demanding them as the basis of a data liberation initiative should speed the revolution:

Structure data immediately as it is entered. Attaching metadata transforms words and numbers into valuable information. It also means that data doesn't have to be constantly re-entered.

This is the single most important step to assure the benefits of data sharing are fully realized. When data is structured (that is, metadata that explains it is attached or mapped to it) the data is given context and is transformed from mere words and into valuable information that can be automatically accessed by any programs and/or machines that recognize that metadata.

That means the data doesn't need to be re-entered, with the resulting risk of error, higher costs, and longer time. Whenever possible, the goal should be a system in which data only needs be entered once and is automatically propagated everywhere. Benefits will include streamlining, coordinating, and automating operations by providing real-time, machine-readable data.

Make data freely available unless there are substantive security and privacy concerns.

The most fundamental change to facilitate liberating data is to make the default presumption in dealing with government and corporate data that it should be shared by those whose roles depend on access to it, rather than assuming it should be kept locked in data bases and access limited. Of course there will be legitimate security and privacy reasons requiring that some data be kept private, but those objections must be legitimate, rather than simply "We've always done it that way."

Unless there are compelling reasons to the contrary, make data available on a real-time, data-in-data-out basis.

Historical data is, of course, important, and should be readily available.

However, data is most valuable when provided on a real-time basis. That is when it can most improve decision-making and analysis by grounding us in current reality. Now that there are relatively low-cost analysis dashboards that will make ubiquitous business intelligence a reality, it is more likely that a growing number of companies and government agencies will begin to provide real-time data streams to their entire workforces, with the exact level of detail and confidential data depending on each individual's role and level of security clearance.

Don't charge for data unless there is a compelling reason to do so.

Data wants to be free, literally and figuratively. In the case of government data, our taxes or fees already paid for its collection, and frequently it is individuals' lives that are the basis for this data. In the past, when entering and retrieving the data was costly and time-consuming, charging for access to data was justifiable. Today it is not.

In the UK and other countries, sale of data, especially geospatial data, is a significant source of income. That should not serve as justification for continuing to charge for data: the potential revenue loss for government is more than offset by potential tax revenues from new services that can be created because of the data.

One positive sign: after the US Open Government Directive was announced, one valuable Health and Human Services Medicare data file that had previously cost $100 and was only available on CD-ROM became available free of charge on the Web.

Make organizations data-centric, with data at the core of their operations and strategy, and with access for all employees determined by their roles.

To fully capitalize on the benefits of access to data, the organization must regard data as at the heart of everything they do. That requires restructuring and managing operations so that data is central, rather than on the periphery: a data-centric organization revolves around its data.

Provide tools to make data understandable and meaningful.

Data is only really valuable when users are able to easily work with it and experiment with it, trying a variety of visualization styles to see which is most illustrative and sharing it with others using Web 2.0 tools.

The "Tools" section of the U.S. Data.gov site, which combines data extraction tools with a variety of widgets, is a good start. However, the best example so far is ManyEyes.com, because it combines a variety of data visualization tools with social media tools such as threaded discussions that will encourage collaborative analysis. Government and corporate sites may be reluctant to host freewheeling discussions of data, so this may remain the province of sites such as Many Eyes.

Protect security and privacy with unified data is simpler than with multiple, fragmentary files.

As we saw with the example of the Beth Israel Deaconess Online Medical Record, unifying data and emphasizing structured data that just only has to be entered once makes it simpler to protect security and privacy than with multiple, fragmentary records. Allowing only permission-based access to parts of these records based on an individual's role and security clearance is much easier to regulate and limit than trying to supervise a wide range of fragmentary databases with varying levels of security.

Make the public and employees trusted partners in using and generating data.

For too long, employees and the public have been given only the data crumbs, not full access, and were discouraged from actively becoming involved in data use and collection. When employees and the public are elevated to the level of full partners in analysis and use of this data, organizations and society will gain the benefit of their individual interests and life experiences. All workers, not just a few élites, should be treated as "knowledge workers" and given access to valuable, real-time data that will help them do their jobs more efficiently.

Build a "data culture", beginning in schools, in which the general public and workforces will be comfortable working with data and have the skills needed to do so.

If people have access to data but don't know how to use it, the data will be wasted. Beginning in the early years of education, expose children to using new data visualization tools and data feeds as part of the curriculum. In the workplace, provide tutorials and opportunity for workers to experiment with data to build their confidence and ability to use it.

Encourage data-centric public policy debate with active involvement from all political perspectives. Encourage discussion of the data, not

just its interpretation.

In the political process, widespread use of, and debate about, data might reduce the level of rancor and make the political process more fact-based and realistic. People and parties on all sides of an issue should be encouraged to monitor data and incorporate it in their deliberations. Debating not just the interpretation of the data but also factors such as assumptions that might color the data itself will improve data quality over time.

Encourage global adoption of data-centric governmental reporting processes to simplify and reduce businesses' costs while facilitating interagency review and improved regulation and public protection.

Tools such as XBRL are free and have been adopted as global standards. Multinational companies that already must report using these standards in one or more countries will be able to amortize their costs if all nations and local governmental entities adopt the same standards.

Allowing companies to file a single structured data file instead of the multiplicity of traditional reports with individual agencies will let them save money while simultaneously improving the quality of regulation, because several agencies can coordinate reviews for the first time. For regulatory reports that are released to the public and corporations, this form of reporting will also allow users to make better comparisons because the reporting standards will be identical for every company.

Encourage rapid spread of liberating data's benefits through open-source

and crowd-sourced applications.

Liberating data has already spread rapidly in part because pioneers have released a variety of apps and widgets created with open source tools, which lowers the cost of creating them. The solutions they create are themselves open source, explicitly inviting others to imitate and improve on the first ones. In this way, global adoption of liberating data will accelerate and poorer governments and their citizens as well as small businesses and individuals will be able to enjoy the benefits as well.

Streamline, coordinate, and automate operations by providing real-time, machine-readable data.

Data that is in "machine-readable," structured formats can automate and drive machinery and devices. This can be a particular boon to businesses, which will be better able to streamline and optimize their operations, while also leading to more devices similar to GPS ones that are automatically updated based on real-time information.

Undoubtedly, in the not-too-distant future we will laugh at how primitive metadata systems such as XBRL were, and how limited the vision of the Semantic Web was.

However, it is likely that two elements of the liberating data revolution will not only remain but also become more powerful in the years to come.

Never again will we believe that data is best carefully controlled.

Any new systems that emerge to structured data will, if anything, increase and simplify the ability to link data and to reuse it seamlessly, further integrating our experiences and globe.

Once set in motion, liberating data can never be reversed, and our world and our lives will be better for it.

ENDNOTES

1) Stephenson, W. David, "Even a role for Twitter in a disaster," W. David Stephenson Blogs on Homeland Security 2.0, August 3, 2007. http://stephensonstrategies.com/2007/08/03/even-a-role-for-twitter-in-a-disaster/

2) Stephenson, W. David, "Democratizing Data: using data feeds and data visualization to drive change." Toronto: New Paradigm, 2008.

3) Siegel, David, Pull, the power of the semantic web to transform your business, New York: Penguin 2009. http://www.amazon.com/Pull-Power-Semantic-Transform-Business/dp/1591842778

4) Stephenson, W. David and Eric Bonabeau, "Expecting the Unexpected: The Need for a Networked Terrorism and Disaster Response Strategy."Homeland Security Affairs III, no. 1 (February 2007) http://www.hsaj.org/?article=3.1.35) The terms liberating data, democratizing data, and open data will all be used interchangeably in this book: all of them deal with giving widespread access to actionable data.

6) Office of the Chief Technology Officer. "Citywide Data Warehouse." http://data.octo.dc.gov/

7) Harris, Blake, "Vivek Kundra: Engineering a Radical Transformation." Digital Communities, March 5, 2009. http://www.govtech.com/dc/articles/625346

8) Peirce, Neal, "A High-Tech Czar's Scorecard." Washington Post Writers Group, March 15, 2009. http://www.postwritersgroup.com/archives/peir090315.htm

9) Collective Insight. "ROI on Apps for Democracy?" Collective Insight blog, Jan. 28, 20089. http://collectiveinsight.net/2009/01/roi-on-apps-for-democracy/

10) U.S. Office of Management and Budget. "Data.gov surpasses 100,000 data sets." News release, July 24, 2009. http://www.whitehouse.gov/omb/blog/09/07/24/DatagovSurpasses100000Datasets/

11) Popularized by Bob Metcalfe, it refers to the concept that the value of a network was proportional to the square of the number of users.

12) http://www.newurbanmechanics.org/

13) The Dutch Taxonomy Project, http://www.xbrl-ntp.nl/english

14) Furchgott, Roy, "It's Your Lipitor on Line 2, The New York Times, April 1, 2009. http://gadgetwise.blogs.nytimes.com/tag/glow-cap/

15) Haisler, Dustin. "QR Codes: how small town Manor, TX is changing government with bar codes." Gov. Fresh, Sept. 18, 2009.

http://govfresh.com/2009/09/qr-codes-how-small-town-manor-texas-is-changing-government-with-barcodes/

16) Let's get the important stuff on the table right away! I pride myself on being a strict constructionist when it comes to grammar and protecting the King's English, and in this case, data is the plural of datum in Latin. However, here's the hard part: it has become common practice to use a singular verb with data and the proper usage sounds a little weird after it's been ignored for so long. So I'll go with the popular usage in this book. In case you're interested, here's the argument: "The word data is the plural of Latin datum, 'something given,' but does that mean you should treat it as a plural noun in English? Not always. The plural usage is still common enough Sometimes scientists think of data as plural, as in These data do not support the conclusions. But more often scientists and researchers think of data as a singular mass entity like information, and most people now follow this in general usage." The American Heritage® Book of English Usage. A Practical and Authoritative Guide to Contemporary English. New York: Random, 1996. I rest my case.

17) Wood, Sarah, "Breaking the Vicious Cycle," Tasty Data Goodies blog, July 14, 2007. http://blog.swivel.com/weblog/2007/07/breaking-the-vi.html

18) Frank DiGiammarino. Interview with author, December 05, 2008.

19) MacCullogh, Diarmaid, The Reformation, a history. New York, 2004, 114.

20) MacCullogh

21) MacCullogh, 147.

22) MacCullogh.

23) MacCullogh, 171.

24) Wendy M. Jameson, CEO, ColnaTec, email to author, March 30, 2009.

25) http://www.guardian.co.uk/activate/video/activate-2010-nigel-shadbolt

26) Definitions of "structured" and "unstructured" data vary. You may find this discussion of interest: http://www.openlinksw.com/blog/~kidehen/?id=991

27) Research and Markets, "US GPS Navigation and Location Based Services Forecast 2010-14," Dublin: August 15, 2010. http://www.satellitemarkets.com/node/696 "World GPS Market Forecast To 2012."

28) Embedded systems are special-purpose computer systems designed to perform a single or a few dedicated functions on a real-time basis, which increasingly drive equipment and processes.

29) Bob Schneider, "The Dutch Taxonomy Project Cuts Red Tape," Data Interactive Blog, March 17, 2007

30) Kundra, Vivek, "Building the Digital Public Square," Oct. 15, 2008. http://www.appsfordemocracy.org/building-the-digital-public-square/

31) Crowdsourcing is the phenomenon in which communities, whether intentional or ad hoc ones, come together using Internet resources, especially open-source software, to accomplish a task collaboratively, with each providing a small portion of the overall solution. Howe, Jeff Crowdsourcing: why the power of the crowd is driving the future of business. New York: Crown Business, 2008.

32) Citywide Data Warehouse, http://dcstat.octo.dc.gov/dcstat/site/default.asp

33) When Kundra launched "Apps for Democracy," he specifically invited other government agencies and good-government groups to launch similar efforts, to encourage "virtuous imitation." Numerous organizations such as the Sunlight Foundation and municipalities such as New York City have followed suit.

34) Eric Gundersen, email to the author, March 17, 2009.

35) Gunderson.

36) "Mash-ups" are developer lingo for applications combining two or more data streams to create more informative data visualizations. such as one combining data on the global spread of influenza cases with another showing the date the first cases were discovered in a given locale.

37) This is the long-tail strategy at work. As detailed by Chris Anderson in his book The Long Tail: Why the Future of Business is Selling Less of More, the long-tail refers to a strategy in which you serve a large aggregate number of customers with products (in this case, data streams) that each serves a small niche.

38) Gundersen.

39) Gundersen.

40) Schneider.

41) Wacoal Case Study, XBRL.org. http://www.xbrl.org/nmpxbrl.aspx?id=90

42) "OCTO Delivers Computers to Every DCPS Classroom," News Release, District of Columbia Office of the Chief Technology Officer, Jan. 31, 2008. http://tinyurl.com/5wkarl

43) Alabama Department of Homeland Security, "Virtual Alabama Fact Sheet," http://www.dhs.alabama.gov/virtual_alabama/home.aspx

44) You can download a free copy of The Beer Game at http://web.mit.edu/jsterman/www/SDG/MFS/simplebeer.html

45) Kelley, Matt, "Some Army surplus unlikely to be used." USA Today, Jan. 12, ,p 5a.

46) Statement by SEC Chairman Christopher Cox, Dec 18, 2008

47) SEC Staff. "21st Century Disclosure Initiative: Staff Report, Modernizing the Securities and Exchange Commission's Disclosure System: Toward Greater Transparency." Securities and Exchange Commission, January, 2009, P. 4.

48) Adelman, Sid, Larissa Moss, Majid Abai, Data Strategy. Boston: Addison-Wesley Professional, 2005.

49) Leskella, Lane. "Economic Crisis and the Dawn of the GRC Era for XBRL." Hitachi Data Interactive Blog, Nov. 13, 2008. http://hitachidatainteractive.com/2008/11/13/economic-crisis-and-the-dawn-of-the-grc-era-for-xbrl/

50) Leskella.

51) Stephenson, W. David, "Automated Data Feeds Make Smart Regulation Possible Now," Huffington Post, September 23, 2008, http://www.huffingtonpost.com/w-david-stephenson/automated-data-feeds-make_b_128208.html

52) Pickert, Kate, "TARP Oversight Report," Time, February 6, 2009

53) While formal definitions of "structured" vs. "unstructured" data vary widely, you may find the Wikipedia definition and discussion

of "unstructured" data helpful. In clarifying this . "Unstructured data," Wikipedia, http://en.wikipedia.org/wiki/Unstructured_data

54) it is precisely because XML is universally recognized and not proprietary that it has been called the Rosetta Stone of data communication. Neil Gross, "A 'Rosetta Stone' for the Web?," Business Week, June 14, 1999. http://www.businessweek.com/1999/99_24/b3633183.htm

55) As XML consultant Neal Hannon puts it, "All reporting comes from the same numbers; one version of the truth." Neal J. Hannon, "Making Data the Center of Your Information System, Strategic Finance, October 2005.

56) Hannon.

57) While Data Dynamite will devote a lot of attention to XBRL, I want to stress that it isn't as critical as the basic concept of tagging the data: doubtless, over time, more powerful tagging systems will replace XBRL, but the tagging concept will still be critical. The XBRL.com site provides an excellent introduction to XBRL "for semi-technical business users." http://www.xbrlsite.com/XBRL_Site/Welcome.html

58) XBRL International, http://www.xbrl.org/

59) "The physical process of tagging with XBRL can be different. In some cases the tagging could be done automatically from probably an accounting system which either understands the tags or someone can make understand the tags." The entire point of XBRL is to make it so a business person can do it. XBRL is kind of like the electronic spreadsheet ... a 'killer app' which made the PC take off. Imagine an XBRL 'spreadsheet' You build what appears to you to be a

spreadsheet, but it is based on not row, column, sheet 'syntax;' but based on business semantics." email from Charles Hoffman to the author, April 11, 2011.

60) Deloitte Touche Tomatsu Australia, "XBRL standards-based financial reporting to bring huge cost savings for business," Sept. 3, 2008. http://www.deloitte.com/view/en_AU/au/press-release/d4dcebf-4c52fb110VgnVCM100000ba42f00aRCRD.htm

61) For a good introduction to the philosophy and practice of open source, see Bruce Perens, Open Sources: Voices from the Open Source Revolution, O'Reilly Media, 1999.

62) As Neal Hannon says, "Business today relies too much on software applications to provide business information and not enough on the data itself (emphasis added)." Hannon.

63) Willis, Mike and Neal J. Hannon, "Combating Everyday Data Problems with XBRL, Part 2," Strategic Finance, August 2005, pp. 59-61

64) Hannon.

65) The Dutch Taxonomy Project, http://www.xbrl-ntp.nl/english

66) Schneider. http:// hitachidatainteractive.com/2007/03/17/the-dutch-taxonomy-project-cuts-red-tape/

67) For consistency, The Dutch have now renamed their process Standard Business Reporting.

68) Standard Business Reporting, "About SBR," http://www.sbr.gov.au/About_SBR.aspx

69) Remarks of FDIC Vice Chairman Martin J. Gruenberg, "XBRL at the FDIC," 14th Annual XBRL International Conference; Philadelphia, December 4, 2006

70) Gruenberg.

71) Gruenberg.

72) Gruenberg.

73) Siegel, 46.

74) Gruenberg.

75) Cox.

76) U.S. Securities and Exchange Commission, "SEC Approves Interactive Data for Financial Reporting by Public Companies, Mutual Funds,News Release, Dec 18, 2008

77) Baker, Neil. "Holland Takes a Different Tack on XBRL," Compliance Week, February 26,2008. http://www.complianceweek.com/article/3978/holland-takes-a-different-tack-on-xbrl

78) Telephone interview with David Fletcher, January 6, 2009.

79) Conversation with author, October 25, 2008.

80) I had this insight while I was an environmental efficiency consultant, and learned that the U.S. Navy's nuclear submarine corps was the first (and perhaps only?) organization to eliminate paper manuals, going to CD-ROMs in the late 1980s. If you're going to be submerged for months at a time, even a single piece of paper takes valuable space, so you'll go to great lengths to eliminate it.

81) Chairing HITSP is particularly relevant to the challenge of universally-accessible and usable data. It involves 500 stakeholder organizations to harmonize standards for clinical summaries, labs, e-prescribing, public health reporting, quality measurement, and personal health records.

82) ANSI News and Publications, "HITSP Chair Dr. Halamka Named Among Top 100 Most Influential in IT," April 30, 2007, http://www.ansi.org/news_publications/news_story.aspx?menuid=7&&articleid=1485

83) Bohmer, Richard M.J., F. Warren McFarlan, Julia Adler-Milstein. "Information Technology and Clinical Operations at Beth Israel Deaconess Medical Center," Cambridge: Harvard Business School, June 14, 2007. N9-607-150

84) BIDC consistently ranks in among the leaders in the annual Most Wired and Most Wireless hospitals surveys by Hospitals && Health Networksmagazine.

85) Bohmer.

86) Unlike some other XML schemas such as XBRL that are global standards, it is US-centric because of some data that is specific to US-based healthcare.

87) Details in Dr. Halamka's blog about how clinical summary records are shared by the Mass. Health Info. Exchange, MA-SHARE, using national standards created by the Healthcare Information Technology Standards Panel (HITSP).

88) Halamka, John D. MD, "New Healthcare Data Standards for the Country," Life as a Healthcare CIO (blog), December 17, 2007. http://geekdoctor.blogspot.com/2007/12/new-healthcare-data-standards-for.html

89) Halamka.

90) Halamka, John D., MD, "Accelerating

Electronic Health Record Adoption," Life As a Healthcare CIO (blog), April 21, 2008. http://geekdoctor.blogspot.com/2008/04/accelerating-electronic-health-record.html

91) Halamka, John D., MD, "Supporting Quality With Information Technology," Life As a Healthcare CIO blog, June 18, 2008. http://geekdoctor.blogspot.com/2008/06/supporting-quality-with-information.html

92) As Halamka told me, if he's treating me in the ER, I want to make sure he has access to every shred of my record, because I may not be able to speak to him and my life may hang in the balance. If, on the other hand, I was a specialist and some parts of my record might not be relevant, then I shouldn't have access to the entire record. This same role-based access limits extend all the way to using basic, anomymized data to report to CDC on communicable diseases and similar issues. (Conversation with the author, December 11, 2008).

93) Few, Stephen C., Show Me the Numbers, Oakland: Analytics Press, 2004, p. 3

94) You owe it to yourself to attend one of Tufte's one-day seminars, offered annually at a variety of sites around the US. Not only do you get to hear him lecture for a day, see first editions of priceless books by Galileo & others, but you also get copies of each of his gorgeous books – worth the price of admission in their own right! For more information: http://edwardtufte.com

95) Tufte, Edward, The Visual Display of Quantitative Information. New Haven: The Graphics Press, 2001, 2nd edition. p.10

96) Many Eyes: http://manyeyes.alphaworks.ibm.com/ Swivel: went out of business during the summer of 2010. Kosara, Robert, "The Rise and Fall of Swivel.com," Ea-gerEyes (blog), October 12, 2010. http://eagereyes.org/criticism/the-rise-and-fall-of-swivel . Pipes: http://pipes.yahoo.com/pipes/. Google Visualization: http://code.google.com/apis/visualization/.

97) Also, don't forget Hannon's comment in the past chapter about how proprietary programs, including data visualization ones, capture and alter data by applying formulas to them. That also applies to proprietary visualization programs.

98) http://en.wikipedia.org/wiki/Social_Data_Analysis Wikipedia

99) As students of emergency response have found, these groups can even be ad hoc ones such as those that spontaneously came together after 9/11 and Katrina and were effective even when official response failed miserably. Stephenson, W. David, "Look to disaster management for Enterprise 2.0 inspiration."Stephenson's Homeland Security 2.0, et.al. (blog), March 24, 2008. http://stephensonstrategies.com/2008/03/24/look-to-disaster-management-for-enterprise-20-inspiration/

100) Busse, Daniella, and Richard Hong., "Business User Empowerment through Collaborative Analytics," Position Paper, CHI 2008 "Social Data Analysis"Workshop, p. 2.

101) Busse, 4.

102) Kosara.

103) "What is Swivel," Tasty Data Goodies (blog,) January 11, 2010. http://blog.swivel.com/weblog/2010/01/what-is-swivel.html

104) Fitzgerald, Brent and Sarah E. Wood. "Social Data Analysis at Swivel: Lessons Learned & Next Steps." http://swivel.com, p. 1.

105) Fitzgerald.

106) http://old.swivel.com/official

107) Cukier, Jérome, "Social Visualization Websites and Official Statistics: The OECD Experience," United Nations Statistical Commission and Economic Commission for Europe, Conference of European Statisticians, (Geneva, 13-15 May 2008). http://unece.org/stats/documents/2008/05/dissemination/wp.4.e.pdf

108) "Overview of ManyEyes," IBM Center for Social Software. http://www.research.ibm.com/social/projects_manyeyes.html

109) Interview with author, Dec. 16, 2008. Wattenberg and co-founder of ManyEyes Fernanda Viégas now work for Google's Big Picture data visualization project.

110) Wattenberg.

111) Barone, Jennifer, "Scientist of the Year Notable: Hans Rosling," Discover Magazine, December 6, 2007. http://discovermagazine.com/2007/dec/hans-rosling

112) Rinehard, Ulrike, "A Data State of Mind," Think Quarterly. http://thinkquarterly.co.uk/01-data/a-data-state-of-mind/

113) Rosling, Hans, "Hans Rosling shows the best stats you've ever seen," TED Talks, Feb. 2006.

114) Barone.

115) Barone.

116) Barone.

117) http://maps.google.com/

118) http://developer.mapquest.com/

119) http://dev.live.com/VirtualEarth/

120) http:// mapnik.org/

121) http://openstreetview.org/

122) The Department of Homeland Security was so impressed with Virtual Alabama that it commissioned a nationwide knock-off, Virtual USA. Bob Greenberg, "Web 2.0 and Homeland Security: States/DHS Launch Virtual USA, " Homeland Security Blog, March 10, 2009. http://www.thehomelandsecurityblog.com/2009/03/10/web-20-and-homeland-security-statesdhs-launch-virtual-usa/

123) Google Enterprise, "Google Earth Enterprise Case Study: Virtual Alabama" video, http://www.youtube.com/watch?v=a-1I0JTWilY

124) Phone interview with the author, March 18, 2009.

125) The site, http://nkla.ucla.edu/, has since vanished without explanation.

126) The NKLA staff took great pains to emphasize they were equally interested in signs of urban vitality and resources. In fact, they armed a group of neighborhood teens with cameras and had them record a wide variety of resources, from story-tellers to wall murals, that were also made part of the project.

127) Pulford,Stephanie, "If Osama Bin Laden Was A Panda, We Could Find Him With Satellites," Scientific Blogging, Feb. 18, 2009. http://www.science20.com/run_and_tumble/if_osama_bin_laden_was_panda_we_could_find_him_satellites

128) Pulford.

129) Chabot, Christian, "Tableau Software's

Chabot: Not Your Father's Business Intelligence," podcast, Jan 5, 2009, http://www.it-financeconnection.com/business-intelligence/not-your-fathers-bi/

130) Botterell, Art. The CAP Cookbook, http://www.incident.com/cookbook

131) Swan Island Networks, "Swan Island Networks Provides 360-Degree-Threat Picture for Super Bowl Security Stakeholders," February 9, 2009, http://www.swanisland.net/news/releases/020909-01.html

132) Surowiecki, James, The Wisdom of Crowds, New York: Doubleday, 2004, xix.

133) According to former OCTO R & D Director Dmitry Kaechev, the effort to make the data available internally to the entire workforce was still more of a goal than a reality when Kundra left. Email to author, March 29, 2009.

134) Fenty was defeated for re-election in 2010, in part because of voter perceptions that he was brilliant but aloof. It remains to be seen if his data reforms will be sustained by his successor, Vincent Gray, who fired Kundra's successor, Bryan Sivak, who also distinguished himself in the job.

135) DISCLAIMER: I served as a consultant to Kudra in the Fall of 2008 to come up with a "blue-sky" plan to make DC the global model for a transparent government. Most of those reforms, however, continue to this day, and the chapter will conclude with a synopsis of new initiatives that OCTO has launched since Kundra left.

136) Email from Dimitry Kaechaev,

137) Kundra, Vivek, interview with the author, Dec. 31, 2008.

138) Kundra. http://www.collaborationpro-ject.org/download/attachments/15073284/Apps+for+Democracy+Vivek+Kundra.pdf?version=1

139) Again, this was more of a goal on Kundra's part than an actual reality by the time he left OCTO.

140) District of Columbia Office of the Chief Technology Officer, "About Citywide Data Warehouse," Citywide Data Warehouse, http://dcstat.octo.dc.gov/dcstat/cwp/view,a,3,q,490374,dcstatNav_GID,1448,dcstatNav,|30935|,.asp

141) Udell, Jon, "Open Government Meets IT," InfoWorld, June 28, 2006. http://www.infoworld.com/d/developer-world/open-government-meets-it-161

142) The District of Columbia, "CAPStat: Building a City That Works," http://capstat.oca.dc.gov/

143) Udell, Jon, "A conversation with Dan Thomas and Suzanne Peck about open government," InfoWorld, Friday, June 23, 2006, weblog.infoworld.com/udell/2006/06/23.html

144) Udell.

145) Udell.

146) Kundra interview.

147) Kundra interview.

148) Eventually OCTO worked with agencies on a "normalization" project to streamline and reduce data errors. The data is still published in XML.

149) Kundra interview. The city's standard "ITSA contract" with IT contractors had such as "baked in measure, so it was easy to start publish ITSA that data.

150) Vivek Kundra, "Testimony," Confirmation hearing on his appointment as chief technology officer of the District of Columbia, City Council Committee on Workforce Development and Government Operations, July 11, 2007

151) Email from Dmitry Kaechaev,

152) Gruman, Galen, "Managing IT as if it were a stock portfolio pushes useful technology to the fore while culling dead-end projects," InfoWorld, June 02, 2008.

153) Gruman.

154) Gruman.

155) DC OCTO, "OCTO Delivers Computers to Every DCPS Classroom," News release, Jan. 31, 2008.

156) DC OCTO, "District of Columbia Launches New Intranet," News release, July 24, 2008

157) OCTO used Twitter and GTalk in addition to conventional means to communicate on a real-time basis during the Inauguration.

158) WJLA-TV News, "D.C. Slashes Red Tape for Simple Building Permits, October 14, 2008.

159) Kundra interview,

160) Kundra interview,

161) Coordination with the District's Chief Purchasing Officer led to OCTO receiving an award from the National Association of State Purchasing Agents.

162) Corbett, Peter, "Apps for Democracy Yeilds (sic) 4,000% ROI in 30 Days for DC.Gov," Nov. 15, 2008 iStrategyLabs blog,

http://www.istrategylabs.com/apps-for-democracy-yeilds-4000-roi-in-30-days-for-dcgov/ Others have questioned the accuracy of the 4,000% ROI (email from Dmitry Kaechaev, op.cit) but, whatever the specifics might be, all acknowledge that Apps for Democracy's benefits far outweighed the costs.

163) Kundra.

164) Burton, Matthew, "Apps for Democracy: an idea for this time and place, " Impublished.org, Nov 22, 2008. http://www.impublished.org/wordpress/apps-for-democracy-an-idea-for-this-time-and-place/

165) Gary Bass, interview with the author, December 12, 2008.

166) Greg Ellin, interview with the author, December 12, 2008. Incidentally, if government takes the initiative to release data rather than activists and the media having to pry it out, agencies will save considerable time and money by minimizing the number of Freedom of Information Act (FOIA) requests to which it must respond.

167) MySociety.org, http://www.mysociety.org/about/

168) FixMyStreets, http://www.mysociety.org./projects/fixmystreets

169) "Sousveillance," http://en.wikipedia.org/wiki/Sousveillance

170) SeeClickFix is an American service that takes the same idea, and allows residents to report various conditions that need fixing to city officials then track the repairs or lack thereof. Boston, Philadelphia, and Dallas are among the communities using it. http://www.seeclickfix.com

171) Lasater, Miles, "SeeClickFix and Respect

to FixMyStreet, June 29, 2009. SeeClick-Fix blog, http://seeclickfix.blogspot.com/2009/06/seeclickfix-and-respect-to-fixmystreet.html

172) WritetoThem.com, http://www.writetothem.com/; HearFromYourMP.com, http://www.hearfromyourmp.com/: TheyWorkForYou.com, http://wwwtheyworkforyou.com

173) Number 10 e-petitions. http://petitions.number10.gov.uk/

174) Tom Steinberg, e-mail to author, Feb.9, 2009.

175) "About the Sunlight Foundation." http://sunlightfoundation.com/

176) Sunlight.

177) Sunlight Labs, http://Sunshine.com

178) Sunlight Labs,

179) "Read the Bill Petition," Read the Bill. Org. http://Readthebill.org/peition

180) Ellen Miller, interview with the author, December 12, 2008.

181) Clay Johnson, interview with the author, December 12, 2008.

182) Sam Adams Alliance. http://www.samadamsalliance.org/

183) "About Us." IllegalSigns.CA. http://illegalsigns.ca/

184) Tabello, Rami. "City Clerk Ulli Watkiss Quietly Introduces New Restrictions on FOI Requesters." IllegalSigns.ca blog, December 4, 2008. illegalsigns.ca/2008/12/04/city-clerk-ulli-watkiss-quietly-introduces-new-restrictions-on-foi-requesters/

185) Roberts, Rob. "Illegal billboards must come down, court rules. National Post blog, February 13, 2009. http://network.nationalpost.com/np/blogs/toronto/archive/2009/02/13/illegal-billboards-must-come-down-court-rules.aspx

186) Dupree, Jacqueline. JDLand. http://www.jdland.com/dc/index.cfm

187) http://www.nytimes.com/2009/04/13/technology/start-ups/13hyperlocal.html

188) Howe, Jeff, "A Coup for Crowdsourced Journalism ...," Crowdsourcing blog, Feb 18, 2008. http://www.google.com/search?q=TPM+crowdsourcing&&start=0&&start=0&&ie=utf-8&&oe=utf-8&&client=mozilla&&rls=org.mozilla:en-US:unofficial

189) Polk award. http://tpmmuckraker.talkingpointsmemo.com/us-attorneys/2007/03/

190) Rep. John Culberson, "The Hill: Culberson posts full health bill online, September 24, 2009. http://culberson.house.gov/the-hill-culberson-posts-full-health-bill-online/

191) Schneider. http://hitachidatainteractive.com/2007/03/17/the-dutch-taxonomy-project-cuts-red-tape/

192) Show Us a Better Way competition, http://www.showusabetterway.com/

193) Power of Information Task Force. "What Would You Create With Public Information?" http://www.showusabetterway.com/

194) Show Us a Better Way. "And the Winners Are." http://www.showusabetterway.co.uk/call/2008/11/and-the-winners-are.html

195) Temple, Adam. "Can I Recycle It?"

http://www.showusabetterway.co.uk/call/2008/07/can-i-recycle-i.html

196) LooFinder. http://www.showusabetterway.co.uk/call/2008/09/loofinder.html

197) "Antisocial behaviour is any aggressive, intimidating or destructive activity that damages or destroys another person's quality of life." Home Office, "Anti-social Behaviour," http://www.homeoffice.gov.uk/anti-social-behaviour/

198) Prime Minister Gordon Brown, "Digital Future" speech, Building Britain's Digital Future Conference, March 22, 2010. http://www.youtube.com/watch?v=0tNkRkPPmOE&&feature=player_embedded

199) Programmer Jeff Gilfelt says it wasn't something inspirational such as being the victim of anti-social behavior that motivated him to create ASBOrometer. In reality, his motivation was quite pragmatic: he was looking for a job and thought this might be a good way to showcase his abilities! Gilfelt, Jeff, "Guest Post: How I built ASBOrometer," Data.gov.UK.

200) "Barack Obama's Speech at Google," Google Blogoscoped, Nov. 19, 2007. http://blogoscoped.com/archive/2007-11-19-n10.html

201) White House Press Office, "Transparency and Open Government," Jan 21,. 2009. http://www.whitehouse.gov/the_press_office/TransparencyandOpenGovernment/

202) Office of the Press Secretary "President Obama Names Vivek Kundra Chief Information Officer, March 5, 2009.

203) "High-value data" was defined as "information that can be used to increase agency accountability and responsiveness; improve public knowledge of the agency and its operations; further the core mission of the agency; create economic opportunity; or respond to need and demand as identified through public consultation."

204) at http://www.[agency].gov/open

205) Sternstein, Aliya, "Obama misses key elements in rolling back secrecy practices," Nextgov, May 28, 2009. http://www.nextgov.com/nextgov/ng_20090528_2864.php

206) Johnson.

207) Ellen Miller, "Success and Setbacks on the Way to a More Open Government" news release, December 7, 2010. http://sunlightfoundation.com/press/releases/2010/12/07/open-government-directive-year-one/

208) StimulusWatch.org. http://stimuluswatch.org

209) Li, Chao. "Stimulus Watch: Where the Money Goes." Buffalo Rising, http://www.buffalorising.com/2009/02/stimulus-watch-where-the-money-goes.html

210) Brito, Jerry. "Preventing Stimulus Waste and Fraud: Who Are the Watchdogs?" testimony before House Committee on Oversight and Government Reform, March 19, 2009. http://www.scribd.com/doc/13406189/Jerry-Brito-Written-Testimony-House-Oversight-Preventing-Stimulus-Waste-and-Fraud?autodown=pdf#document_metadata

211) Even more upsetting, the government gave a company an $18.5 million contract to upgrade the site – money that could have been spent on substance rather than style. "Recovery.gov Chief Downplays Criticism," Daily Tech Dose, National Journal, July 10, 2009. http://techdailydose.nationaljournal.com/2009/07/recoverygov-chief-

downplays-cr.php

212) Stephenson, W. David. "Recovery. gov: the First Step Toward Smart Regulation?" Huffington Post, February 23, 2009. http://www.huffingtonpost.com/w-david-stephenson/recoverygov-the-first-ste_b_168555.html

213) O'Brien, Tim. "Vivek Kundra: Federal CIO in His Own Words," O'Reilly Radar blog, March 5, 2009. http://radar.oreilly.com/2009/03/vivek-kundra-federal-cio-in-hi.html

214) Robinson, David, Harlan Yu, William P Zeller, && Edward T. Felton. "Government Data and the Invisible Hand." Yale Journal of Law &&Technology, 160 (2009)

215) "Community," Data.gov. http://data.gov

216) Jackson, Joab, "Molly O'Neill Web 2.0 the EPA Way," Government Computer News, Jan. 29, 2008. http://gcn.com/Articles/2008/01/29/Molly-ONeill–EPA-the-Web-20-way.aspx?p=1

217) I had also advocated use of XBRL to report TARP spending. In fact I argued that since it was the public's money, tagging the reports with XBRL could and should allow real-time reporting of use of the money, which was justified also because of the instability of the US economy at the time. With XBRL, quarterly reporting is outmoded: companies could simply do it automatically as they go about their business. Sternstein, Aliya, "Lack of Reporting, Communication Threatens TARP Program, " NextGov, March 31, 2009. http://www.nextgov.com/nextgov/ng_20090331_4220.php

218) Issa, Rep. Darrell, "Technology is key to achieving 21st century transparency in government," Washington Examiner, October 25, 2010.

219) Mosley, Ray, "Federal Register 2.0: Opening a Window onto the Inner Workings of Government," Open Government Initiative Blog, October 5, 2009. http://www.whitehouse.gov/blog/Federal-Register-20-Opening-a-Window-onto-the-Inner-Workings-of-Government/

220) Lee, Tom, "Meet the New Federal Register," Sunlight Labs Blog, July 26, 2010. http://www. sunlightlabs.com/blog/2010/meet-the-new-federal-register/

221) IBM, "Smarter Planet Overview: Instrumented. Intelligent. Interconnected." http://www.ibm.com/smarterplanet/us/en/overview/ideas/index.html?lnk=ibmhpls1/smarterplanet/overview/mobile

222) Dr. Colin Harrison, conversation with the author, March 18, 2011.

223) The first phase of Masdar City was supposed to be completed in 2009, but the scale of the project was reduced and the timelines extended because of the global economic crisis. The first phase is now planned to be completed in 2015. http://en.wikipedia.org/wiki/Masdar_City

224) Harrison.

225) Banawar, Guru S., "Building Smarter Smaller Cities," Building a Smarter City blog, December, 13th 2010.

226) Banawar.

227) In November, 2010, Haisler became the director of government innovation for Spigit, a Web 2.0 "collaborative idea management software" company whose products he'd used in Manor. http://www.marketwire.com/press-release/Spigit-

Welcomes-Dustin-Haisler-as-Director-of-Government-Innovation-1345261.htm He remains an advisor to the City of Manor.

228) "How Do QR Codes Work?" http://www.qrme.co.uk/qr-codes-explained.html

229) Haisler. http://govfresh.com/2009/09/qr-codes-how-small-town-manor-texas-is-changing-government-with-barcodes/

230) American Society for Quality, "Plan-Do-Check-Act Cycle." http://asq.org/learn-about-quality/project-planning-tools/overview/pdca-cycle.htmlss

231) iSixSigma, "What is Six Sigma?" http://www.isixsigma.com/index.php?option=com_k2&&view=item&&id=1463:what-is-six-sigma?&&Itemid=107

232) Boyd, John, "The Essence of Winning and Losing," slide presentation, 1995. http://www.danford.net/boyd/essence4.htm

233) Senge, Peter M., The Fifth Discipline: the art of the learning organization, (New York: Crown Business, 1996 [revised edition]). 3.

234) Gartner Research, "Now is the time for the Zero-Latency Enterprise," http://www.gartner.com/pages/story.php.id.2632.s.8.jsp

235) Siegel, 11.

236) Fingar, Peter and Joseph Bellini, The Real-Time Enterprise, (Tampa: Meghan-Kiffer Press, 2004 [Galley Proof]). 30.

237) Jamie Biggar, e-mail exchange with the author, June 11, 2010.

238) Although it's important to note that the data will not have to reside in a mono-lithic central data warehouse: one of the beauties of structured data is that will literally reside where it was first entered, but because of structured data's ability to automatically flow anywhere it is needed, a single piece of data can both remain where it was entered and simultaneously be at the heart of everything the company does.

239) "Data, data everywhere," The Economist, February 10, 2010.

240) Michael Grean and Michael Shaw, "Supply-Chain Partnership between P & G and Wal-Mart," E-Business Management Integrated Series in Information Systems, 2002, Volume 1, 10.

241) Grean, 17.

242) Grean, 13.

243) An Internet Protocol address (IP Address) is a unique numerical label assigned to any device that's part of a computer network using Internet Protocol to communicate between parts of the network.

244) http://www.senseaware.com/SA/index.html

245) MacManus, Richard, "FedEx Joins the Internet of Things with SenseAware," ReadWriteWeb, December 4, 2009. http://www.readwriteweb.com/archives/fedex_joins_the_internet_of_things_with_senseaware.php

246) McManus. http://www.readwriteweb.com/archives/fedex_joins_the_internet_of_things_with_senseaware.php

247) McManus.

248) Walllace, Amy, "Putting Customers in Charge of Design," The New York Times, May 15, 2010. http://www.nytimes.

com/2010/05/16/business/16proto.html

249) Tapscott, Don and Anthony R. Williams, Wikinomics: how mass collaboration changes everything. New York: Portfolio, 2006

250) 480,189 users rated 17,770 movies , creating the 100,480,507 recommendations. The records were scrubbed of any personal identifiers and identified only by a number to protect users' anonymity. However, an anonymous Netflix user later sued Netflix, alleging that releasing the datasets violated U.S. fair trade laws and the Video Privacy Protection Act. Letter from Greg McAlpin in response to Omar Gallaga's column about his presentation at SXSW. Gallaga, Omar L. Panel: "Crowdsourcing: The Ensemble's Experience With the Netflix Prize, " March 25, 2010.http://www.austin360. com/blogs/content/shared-gen/blogs/ austin/digitalsavant/entries/2010/03/25/ sxsw_panel_crow.html

251) http://audio.sxsw.com/2010/podcasts/Interactive/2010-03-13/Crowdsourcing-The-Ensembles-Experience-With-the-Netflix-Prize.mp3Netflix Competition

252) "Crowdsourcing, The Ensemble's Experience"

253) Van Buskirk, Eliot," "How the Netflix Prize Was Won,"Wired, Sept. 22, 2009. http:// www.wired.com/epicenter/2009/09/how-the-netflix-prize-was-won/#ixzz11Xg6GmIP

254) McAlpin, Greg, "Crowdsourcing: The Ensemble's Experience With the Netflix Prize, " SXSW 2010 podcasts. http://sxsw. com/node/5003

255) Gravity Technologies, Netflix Prize, http://www.gravityrd.com/gravity/news_ list.php?newsgroupid=4&&gravity=netflix

&&lang=en

256) Siegel, 46.

257) I have argued that this should be done for loans under the TARP program. Sternstein, "Lack of reporting, communication threaten TARP program." http://www.nextgov.com/nextgov/ng_20090331_4220.php Siegel,

258) Sadly, in my conversations with leaders in the global XBRL community, they report that most companies are only adding the tags to their conventionally-prepared reporting documents. That's a lose-lose situation: they incur additional costs for tagging the data, and totally miss out on the benefits!

259) Siegel, 47.

260) Hasegawa, Morikuni, Taiki Sakata, Nobuyuki Sambuichi, Neal Hannon (CMA); "Breathing New Life into Old Systems with XBRL GL, " Strategic Finance, March 2004. 46-51.

261) Hasegawa.

262) Actually, referring to a handful of companies that "get it" about XBRL and actually implement it for anything beyond regulatory reporting is being charitable. The only other one I could find is Fujitsu: http://18thconference.xbrl.org/ sites/18thconference.xbrl.org/files/hanaoka.pdf

263) Ambient Devices, "Information Cognition." http://www.ambientdevices.com/cat/ science.html

264) Ambient Devices, http://www.ambientdevices.com/cat/orb/PGE.html

265) Ambient Devices, "My Ambient,"

https://www.myambient.com/account/login

266) Ambient Devices, "The Ambient Umbrella," http://www.ambientdevices.com/products/umbrella.html

267) Cooney, Elizabeth, "Study urges action to get patients to follow prescriptions, The Boston Globe, August 14, 2009. http://www.boston.com/news/local/massachusetts/articles/2009/08/14/study_urges_action_to_get_patients_to_follow_prescriptions/

268) Wagner, Mitch, "Medicine Bottles Get Net Connection," Information Week, November 20, 2009.

269) Higginbotham, Stacey, "Ericsson CEO Predicts 50 Billion Internet Connected Devices by 2020," GigaOM, April 14, 2010. http://gigaom.com/2010/04/14/ericsson-sees-the-internet-of-things-by-2020/

270) "The Difference Engine: Chattering objects," The Economist, Aug 13th 2010.

271) Kelleher, Kevin, "The Wired 40," Wired, July 2003. http://www.wired.com/wired/archive/11.07/40main.html

272) LePatner, Barry B., "The industry that time forgot," The Boston Globe Ideas section, August 12, 2007. http://www.boston.com/news/globe/ideas/articles/2007/08/12/the_industry_that_time_forgot/

273) Katel, Peter. "Bordering on Chaos: The Cemex Story," Wired, May 1997. http://www.mexconnect.com/articles/639-the-cemex-story

274) Carrying the pizza analogy even farther, "To promote the offer, Cemex has even printed miniature pizza boxes labeled with a slogan that pokes a little fun at the local Domino's franchise: Now, the concrete is faster than the pizza."

275) Katel.

276) Personal Informatics, http://personalinformatics.org/

277) Data.Gov, Geodata catalogue. http://www.data.gov/catalog/geodata

278) "Flightview," http://www.flightview.com/

279) Ravnitsky, Michael, "The Postman Always Pings Twice," The New York Times, December 18, 2010. http://www.nytimes.com/2010/12/18/opinion/18ravnitzky.html

280) Wortham, Jenna. "Foursquare Signs a Deal With Zagat." New York Times, February 9, 2010. http://bits.blogs.nytimes.com/2010/02/09/foursquare-inks-a-deal-with-zagat/

281) Stephenson, W. David. "Fight Terror With Palm Pilots." The Boston Globe, October 30, 2001.

282) Starks, Tim. "Will That Pocketbook Get You Dragged Out of Line at JetBlue? Palm's E-Based Hazards Checklist Can Help." CQ Homeland Security: Product of the Week, Oct. 14, 2003

283) Coxe, Christopher. Statement, SEC Board Meeting, Dec. 17, 2008. http://www.sec.gov/news/speech/2008/spch121708ccidata.wmv

284) Department of Health and Human Services, Hospital Quality Compare, http://www.hospitalcompare.hhs.gov

285) For a variety of other early examples of the phenomenon, especially as it relates to chronicling personal experiences, see

Brophy-Warren, Jamin. "The New Examined Life: Why more people are spilling the statistics of their lives on the Web," Wall Street Journal, Dec. 6, 2008. http://online.wsj.com/article/SB122852285532784401.html

286) National Audubon Society, "History." http://www.audubon.org/bird/cbc/history.html

287) "Current Year Results." http://cbc.audubon.org/cbccurrent/current_table.html Some of the 2009 lists were compiled on iPhones using Audubon's new Audubon Guide Apps

288) National Audubon Society,"How CBC Helps Birds." http://www.audubon.org/bird/cbc/howcbchelpsbirds.html

289) Arrington, Michael. "Search for Steve Fossett extends to Amazon's Mechanical Turk." TechCrunch, Sept. 8, 2007. http://techcrunch.com/2007/09/08/search-for-steve-fossett-expands-to-amazons-mechanical-turk/

290) Williams, Anthony. "Crowdsourcing versus citizen science," Wikinomics blog, February 9, 2009. http://www.wikinomics.com/blog/index.php/2009/02/09/crowdsourcing-versus-citizen-science/comment-page-1/

291) Muzzin, Suzanne Taylor. "Researcher's project lures citizen 'scientists' into other galaxies." Yale University Office of Public Affairs, Feb. 20, 2009.

292)

293) Miller, Terrie. Citizen Science Blog. http://citizensci.com

294) "Mobile app sees science go global." BBC News, Sept. 16, 2009. http://news.bbc.co.uk/2/hi/science/nature/8258501.stm

295) Stephenson and Bonabeau.

296) Stephenson, W. David. "Fight Terror With Palm Pilots." The Boston Globe, October 10, 2001.

297) I call this "digital triage": siphoning off some people so that first responders could concentrate their efforts on those in most need of help.

298)

299) EPIC, "Helping Haiti: Tweak the Tweet: propagate the specialized tweet syntax. http://epic.cs.colorado.edu/helping_haiti_tweak_the_twe.html

300) Augmented Environments Laboratory, Georgia Tech. "The Voices of Oakland." http://www.cc.gatech.edu/ael/projects/voicesofoakland.html

301) "Historic European Locales Resurrected On Augmented Reality Tours," ScienceStage.com http://sciencestage.com/resources/historic-european-locales-resurrected-augmented-reality-tours

302) Pescovitz, David. "The Quantified Self: You Are Your Data." Good.is, Feb. 3, 2009. http://www.good.is/post/the-quantified-self-you-are-your-data/

303) smartphones don't have built-in CO_2 monitors, so "PEIR uses GPS technology to determine the values indirectly. As you go about your routine — jogging, commuting, running errands — your mobile phone uses GPS and cell towers to record and upload your location every few seconds to your secure profile. Based on this location trace, the system infers your activity (walking, biking, driving, riding the bus) and logs it throughout the day."

304) I highly recommend that you watch the "Participatory Sensing" video about PEIR to really grasp how it integrates so many data sources: http://j.mp/bQpVCQ

305) McClusky, Mark. "The Nike Experiment: How the Shoe Giant Unleashed the Power of Personal Metrics," Wired, June 22, 2009. http://www.wired.com/medtech/health/magazine/17-07/lbnp_nike

306)

307) Dolan, Brian, "Korea Telecom pilots mobile-enabled diabetes management," MobiHealthNews, Apr 12, 2011. http://mobihealthnews.com/10698/korea-telecom-pilots-mobile-enabled-diabetes-management/

308) Blackman, Andre. "Interview with Alexandra Carmichael of CureTogether." Vimeo, Oct. 21, 2009. http://vimeo.com/7193624

309)

310) PatientsLikeMe, http://www.patientslikeme.com/

311) District of Columbia Office of the Chief Technology Officer. "Apps for Democracy Medal Winners, "http://www.appsfordemocracy.org/apps-for-democracy-medal-winners/

312) I guess, in light of IBM's "Watson," that I should add a disclaimer: they can't handle ambiguity... yet!

313) Berners-Lee, Tim, The Next Web of Open, Linked Data," TED Talks, March 3, 2009. http://blog.ted.com/2009/03/13/tim_berners_lee_web/

314) "Data, Data Everywhere," The Economist, Feb 5, 2010.

315) "Monstrous Amounts of Data," The Economist, Feb. 5, 2010.

316) The Economist, "Data, Data Everywhere."

317) "Chromogram," IBM Visual Communication Lab. Wikipedia comment Chromogram. "Light green comments start with "geography" as the user mentions the maps he has added to each article of a given town."

318) "Merrill Lynch estimates that more than 85 percent of all business information exists as unstructured data – commonly appearing in e-mails, memos, notes from call centers and support operations, news, user groups, chats, reports, letters, surveys, white papers, marketing material, research, presentations and Web pages." Blumberg, Robert, Shaku Atre, "The Problem With Unstructured Data," Information Management Magazine, February 2003, http://www.information-management.com/issues/20030201/6287-1.html

319) One of the things that gives me cause for optimism is the spontaneous behavioral change by social media users when tagging content was introduced. I am unaware of any formal programs to train users, yet people quickly learn first to use the tags, and then quickly learn to refine their use to be as efficient as possible. Given that intuitive behavior, I can't help thinking that it should be possible to expand upon that base and, over time, increase the percentage of Web content that is structured simply because users realize it is in their self-interest to do so. An effective online education program could speed that transition.

320) Sunlight Labs. "Apps for America 2: The Data.gov Challenge." http://www.sunlightlabs.com/contests/appsforamerica2/

321) Forum One Networks. "Forum One's DataMasher Places in the Top Three Finalists in the 'Apps for America 2' Contest." Aug. 26, 2009. http://www.forumonenetworks.com/content/article/detail/3452/>

322) Sliedan, Johann, "Address to the Estates of the Empire," quoted in Eisenstein, Elizabeth L., "The Role of the Printing Press in the Reformation," The Reformation, San Diego: Greenhaven Press, 1999. 84-5.

323) Ironic historical footnote in light of the 95 Theses' historical impact: no one attended the public meeting Luther hosted to discuss them! Marty, Martin. Martin Luther. New York: Lipper-Viking, 2004. p. 33.

324) Expanding on the basic principles of liberating data given in Ch. 1.

INDEX

ABOUT THE AUTHOR

W. DAVID STEPHENSON

W. David Stephenson earned an international reputation as a Gov./Enterprise 2-3.0 strategist and theorist. He particularly focuses on organizational data transformation strategies and homeland security and disaster management.

His "networked homeland security" strategy capitalizes on the combination of advanced mobile devices and social network apps to make the public full partners in preparation and response. Stephenson created app suites putting information necessary to prepare for and/or respond to disasters in easy-to-use form for smartphones.

Stephenson is a frequent speaker on innovation at e-government, Web 2-3.0, and homeland security conferences worldwide. His expertise also includes organizational transformation through Web 2-3.0, corporate issue management, and new economic and environmental visions. His articles on data liberation, governmental transparency, homeland security, crisis management, new economic paradigms, and advanced technology have appeared in publications and online.

Before entering the Web 2.0 field, Stephenson provided award-winning crisis management, community relations, and public relations services plus Web strategies in the environmental, energy and health care fields. He drafted and won passage of the Massachusetts law requiring labeling of plastic packaging to encourage its recycling.

Stephenson began his career as an associate producer and writer of award-winning documentaries at WCVB-TV. He was speechwriter, assistant press secretary and press secretary to former Massachusetts Governor Michael Dukakis. He earned a B.A. from Haverford College and a M.A. from the Newhouse School at Syracuse University, where he was a University Fellow.

....

ABOUT THE COVER

The cover was adapted from a photograph by Chris Jordan, who specializes in eye-catching, thought-provoking data visualizations. This one, "E Pluribus Unum," was 24' x 24', laser-etched onto aluminum panels. It depicts the names of one million organizations globally that are devoted to peace, environmental stewardship, social justice, and preservation of diverse and indigenous culture. According to Jordan, "Despite their enormous diversity of size, focus, and geographic location, they are all united around a set of core values that places compassion and stewardship as highest priorities....I think of this piece as being like a compass, pointing toward a true source of hope and inspiration for our times." www.chrisjordan.com

www.ingramcontent.com/pod-product-compliance
Lightning Source LLC
Chambersburg PA
CBHW072125270326
41931CB00010B/1677

9 7 8 0 9 8 3 6 4 9 0 0 7